D0478360

ALSO BY ISAAC CRONIN

THE INTERNATIONAL
SQUID COOKBOOK

THE CALIFORNIA
SEAFOOD COOKBOOK

EATING FOR TWO:
THE COMPLETE PREGNANCY
NUTRITION COOKBOOK

CHAMPAGNE!

THE NEW AMERICAN
VEGETABLE COOKBOOK

THE
MINDFUL
COOK

FINDING

AWARENESS,

SIMPLICITY,

AND FREEDOM

IN THE

KITCHEN

VILLARD   NEW YORK

THE
MINDFUL
COOK

ISAAC CRONIN

All rights reserved under International and Pan-American Copyright Conventions.
Published in the United States by Villard Books, a division of Random House, Inc.,
New York, and simultaneously in Canada by Random House of Canada Limited,
Toronto.

Grateful acknowledgment is made to Macmillan General Reference USA for
permission to reprint "Tomato Chutney" from *A Taste of India* by Madhur Jaffrey.
Copyright © 1985 by Madhur Jaffrey. Reprinted by permission of Macmillan General
Reference USA.

VILLARD BOOKS and colophon are registered
trademarks of Random House, Inc.

Library of Congress Cataloging-in-Publication Data

Cronin, Isaac.
     The mindful cook: finding awareness,
simplicity, and freedom in the kitchen / Isaac Cronin.
          p.   cm.
     Includes bibliographical references.
     ISBN 0-375-50275-0
     1. Cookery. 2. Food. I. Title.
   TX652.C8323   1999
   641.5—dc21   99-20374

Random House website address:
www.atrandom.com

Printed in the United States of America on
acid-free paper

98765432

First Edition

Book design by Barbara M. Bachman
Illustrations by Nicole Kaufman

ACKNOWLEDGMENTS

Olivia Blumer, agent, for effortless agenting and a much needed reality check; David Cronin, father, for showing me that cooking is a passion worthy of a man's attention; Herman Graf, friend and potential publisher, for making me an offer I could refuse, and therefore encouraging me to hold out for a better one; Nevin Schreiner, friend, for bolstering me in moments of doubt, and for introducing me to Mitch; Terrel Seltzer, journey partner, for encouraging me to take risks even at her own peril; Mitch Sisskind, collaborator, for providing incisive editing and clear focus at every stage of the process; Bruce Tracy, editor, for helping me to discover that a book has its own life and identity to which we are beholden.

CONTENTS

INTRODUCTION

Preparing food is a basic human activity. It's essential in the true sense of the word. It touches on the essence of ourselves as social beings—and rituals of preparing and serving food are among the most significant measures of any culture's level of genuine civilization. That was true when the banquet traditions of Rome and medieval Europe were at their height, and it's true in our own era of supermarkets and convenience foods.

Today cooking and eating are characterized by two social trends. First, there is an emphasis on convenience and time saving as ends in themselves. There is also a focus on appearance—how food looks is as important or more important than how it tastes, smells, or how it was prepared. As these tendencies gain acceptance, they move us further and further away from a respect for the core human experience of cooking, that is, the transformation of raw ingredients into physical, emotional, and even spiritual nourishment.

The purpose of this book is to help you rediscover the authenticity of preparing and enjoying food, an experience that is deeply inherent in our nature. As children, we luxuriated in the taste and texture of ice cream. We carefully skewered a hot dog on a stick and held it over a fire until it was charred in exactly the right way. We recognized the importance of holiday meals not only through the oohing and ahhing over the chocolate cake as it was brought to the table, but also in the preceding act of baking that included licking the beaters, melting the chocolate, whipping the cream, and so on.

The Mindful Cook is about reawakening spontaneity and childlike wonder in your relationship to food. It's about seeing, touching, and tasting food again as if for the first time, and in the chapters that follow we'll use a simple but powerful technique for reframing these experiences. In a word, the technique is *mindfulness.* Through mindful awareness, limiting preconceptions will be identified. Constraining habits will be extinguished. Most important, lost passions will be rediscovered.

As you take the practical journey of the Mindful Cook laid out in these pages, you will experience the act of cooking in a different way. Being in the kitchen will gradually become *being* in the kitchen. All this is within your reach if you allow yourself to focus on it.

THE
MINDFUL
COOK

CHAPTER ONE

WHAT IS
A MINDFUL
COOK?

Many people enjoy cooking. Others hate and fear it. This book is for people who want to learn how to love it. According to a recent article in *The New York Times,* buyers of new luxury homes are insisting on large, well-appointed kitchens, not only to demonstrate they can afford them, but to emphasize the importance of good food in their lives. Few of these people actually cook. Although most would like to, their confidence level does not match their good intentions.

Right now, you may feel close to helpless in the kitchen. Or you may exert such tight control that preparing a meal resembles a military campaign with the recipe serving as the general's war plan and the pots and pans acting as the artillery and the infantry. You may be so intimidated by cooking that even on a dare you would never attempt anything beyond a hamburger or a grilled cheese sandwich. Or, conversely, you may look disdainfully upon "simple food" as the province of simple people. Whatever dire impulse or inhibition may afflict you in the kitchen, this book can help you replace it with freedom, focus, and genuine fun. That's what being a Mindful Cook really means.

In the pages that follow, the word *mindfulness* draws on two traditions, one rooted in Eastern spiritual practice and the other in Western psychology. Meditation, for example, as practiced in Zen or yoga, creates a quality of heightened inner awareness that coexists with deep relaxation and freedom from everyday anxieties. There are many ways to achieve this condition, including physical exercise, physical stillness, concentration on a complex visual pattern or a repetition of a brief sequence of meaningless syllables—and even through food preparation, as in the Japanese tea ceremony. Once a person has become skilled at entering and maintaining the meditative state, he or she benefits not only in terms of spiritual growth but also in an ability to function more effectively in the world.

In the United States, a somewhat different definition of mindfulness has been the subject of many years of research by Dr. Ellen Langer, a professor of psychology at Harvard University. Langer's studies center on the benefits of focused awareness on an activity, and on the negative influences of feelings such as fear, haste, and simple absentmindedness, which can distort perceptions and impede performance. The Mindful Cook respects both Eastern and Western interpretations, and proposes that both can be brought to life in the kitchen.

Yes, it's true: You can nourish your soul, develop your mind, and eat well at the same time! Mindful cooking is not a matter of executing complicated recipes or impressing a dining room full of dinner guests. In fact, the Mindful Cook is as engaged by boiling an egg as by baking a ten-layer cake. He or she cooks for one person or for a dozen with equal attention and satisfaction. Most important, the Mindful Cook fully experiences whatever happens with a unique combination of awareness and detachment. Regardless of the temperature in the kitchen, the Mindful Cook stays cool.

Mindfulness, then, is a quality of spirit, but it's also an eminently effective approach to preparing food. The spiritual essence of *The Mindful Cook* is really at one with the book's practical foundation. From both points of view, there's an understanding that qualities of the mind and heart in cooking are just as important or more important than the oven or the refrigerator. This is not abstract doctrine. It's simply the most effective approach to becoming a good cook—someone who makes nourishing food and enjoys every moment of the process.

I've come to these realizations by a circuitous route. Children love kitchens, and growing up I was no exception. In this most marvelous of rooms there was fire, and water, and drawer after drawer full of strange implements—eggbeaters, potato mashers, spatulas, corkscrews—most of them harmless but carrying just a hint of danger. This amazing room was simply the best of all possible worlds: a peaceful and reassuring place, but exciting at the same time. As I recall, the surprises were endless. The kitchen was in many ways the household version of the mad scientist's laboratory, an edible chemistry set, where the wildest research could be undertaken, where creations could be sampled, catalogued, and consumed in one place.

I became one of those men, moreover, for whom the allure of the kitchen in no way diminished over time. On the contrary, food and cooking have remained extremely important elements in my life. At various times I've been a farmer, a fisherman, a writer of cookbooks, a caterer, a food columnist for major newspapers, and a kind of Johnny Appleseed popularizer of new ingredients. For me, food has been not only a source of sustenance, but also a medicine, an artistic medium, and a vehicle for gentle social change.

Yet despite the intensity of my involvement with food, something was never quite right. I knew this and, unfortunately, so did anyone who came near me while I was cooking.

In the kitchen, I saw myself as a warrior. The stove, the refrigerator, and the countertops were my battlefields. Here I struggled to the finish against the forces of nature. Whenever a guest came to dinner—and there were years when this happened several times a week—nothing short of six-course perfection would suffice. My family stayed clear of me as I completed my gastronomic masterpieces. I was always in a hurry, I couldn't take a joke, and there were plenty of dirty dishes. While my guests had a great time (as long as they arrived after I had finished preparing the meal), I suffered from a case of performance anxiety that wouldn't quit. The more I did, the more reasons I had to worry.

When I began teaching cooking classes, I noticed that one question came up again and again in different forms. How can I become comfortable in the kitchen? How do I live with the reality that something is always going to go wrong? It soon dawned on me that although I might be a somewhat inventive cook, I had never felt relaxed in the kitchen. I was always too busy proving myself. I was underperforming by overperforming.

In a way, this was perfectly understandable. We live in a world that is results-oriented. Earning a handsome salary; producing attractive, intelligent children; creating a successful church-based charity; reaching a ripe old age; dressing with style; shooting a low golf score; and preparing elegant, delicious dinners for friends are the kind of accomplishments that many of us strive for. We are judged by what we produce, by what others can see that we have accomplished in tangible terms. *How* we achieve the goal is not nearly as important as the fact that we have accomplished it. Somehow the experience of the journey is lost in the evaluation of the result.

As I began to see all this more clearly, I took a step back from professional cooking. Getting away from the daily routine of recipe testing and writing allowed me to focus on some fundamental questions. How could someone really learn to cook? Did the end justify the means? Was cooking even something that could be learned, or was it simply a gift that you either have or you don't?

When the answers began to appear, they were in the form

of other questions. What is the real definition of cooking, for example? Well, to nourish the cook and those who share the food he or she prepares. And what is nourishment? Certainly it is more than just vitamins; otherwise why was I going to all this trouble? Cooking can be appreciated as a process, therefore, more than a presentation. Once I allowed myself to focus on the journey in the kitchen rather than a mental image of a perfect result, I gradually began to experience a new kind of pleasure as I prepared food. I could cook for cooking's own sake. Cooking, seemingly the most goal-oriented of activities—because we literally must eat to survive—could nevertheless be experienced as an end in itself. The activity could be its own reward. This was the true inner "joy of cooking" rediscovered. And, almost paradoxically, I now found myself inspired to produce results that others seem to enjoy even more.

The Mindful Cook is a distillation of these revelations. It is less a cookbook than a cooking book, which is why it is not filled with a lot of recipes. Its purpose is not the creation of perfect dishes, but the ongoing development of awareness and enjoyment in you, the reader and the cook. The book encourages you to become more at home in the kitchen through appreciation of the rhythms of cooking, the textures of ingredients, and the thousand other pleasures that are always available regardless of how the meal turns out.

While many books remind us "you are what you eat," in these pages I suggest that we are how we cook. This approach refers not only to the techniques of preparing a dish, but also to your thoughts and feelings as you plan a meal, shop for the ingredients, and put it on the table.

This view of cooking as a self-fulfilling activity leads directly to the idea of cooking as a kind of meditation or spiritual activity. Throughout history cooking and eating have been understood as sacred experiences, and *The Mindful Cook* seeks to renew the intimate connection between spirituality and food. Again, this also has a practical intention. By making use of meditations from the diverse traditions of Zen Buddhism, Taoism, and Indian mythology, we can find exciting new ways of working in the kitchen.

Today more than ever before, the center of the American home is the kitchen. In part this is due to a vague feeling that the act of cooking should have profound meaning in our lives, but the actual, concrete experience of this richness is becoming increasingly rare. *The Mindful Cook* takes American's obsessive interest in food as its starting point and builds on that concern to explore cooking in a new way—one that's somehow playful and reverent simultaneously. This, I'm pleased to discover, is not unlike how I remember feeling about the kitchen in the first place.

I know this approach can work because it has been the experience of my own life. Rather than a spiritual person who discovered cooking, I am a cooking person who has been led through the kitchen to an awareness of the importance and practical significance of spirituality. In *The Mindful Cook,* I invite you to share my journey.

MINDFUL PRACTICE

Each chapter in this book contains four practical moments:

1. "A Mindful Look" is an inquiry into your culinary self that takes the form of a series of questions. These are queries with no right or wrong answers. They are intended to open avenues of consideration regarding your individual approach to food.
2. "A Mindful Step" takes the form of an exercise, because the focus of this book is eminently practical.
3. "On the Horizon" offers additional practical challenges that deepen and intensify some of the themes developed in "A Mindful Step." They can be pursued now as an immediate extension of the process, or on a return to the mindful path at some other time.
4. A recipe (or recipes) that focuses the issues raised in the chapter and transforms them into something wonderful to eat through the magic of cooking.

Because the Mindful Cook pays equal attention to every aspect of food and cooking, because choosing food, readying the kitchen, cooking the ingredients, and serving are indivisible parts of the same process, we will devote as much attention to the before and after of preparing food as to the act of cooking itself. The act of cooking becomes the center in Chapter 6. Before then it is an intent that gradually comes into focus.

The gate is open. Let's go in.

A MINDFUL LOOK

As a way of beginning the path toward more mindful cooking, create a realistic appraisal of your strengths and, more important, your weaknesses in the kitchen. Write down the answers to these and the other questions in this book so that you can refer back to them when you have completed the other exercises, or a year from now when you want to check your progress.

1. How do you picture yourself when you cook? Are you relaxed, anxious, hurried, preoccupied? Create a one hundred–word portrait of your kitchen persona, listing several things you like and don't like about cooking.
2. How do you imagine others perceive you when you are cooking? Ask a few of your friends or family members to confirm or correct this perception.
3. What do you see as the major obstacles to being more comfortable and effective in the kitchen? Include in this list hang-ups, fears, preoccupations, and practical limitations.

A MINDFUL STEP

Select a friend or relative or someone you have seen in action whose kitchen presence you admire. Try to articulate exactly what he does in the kitchen that pleases you. Create a simple plan to emulate some aspect of his behavior, such as his willingness to recruit guests to help with kitchen tasks, his calm under fire, or his modesty. Don't just borrow his recipes; appropriate some pleasing aspect of his attitude. Concentrate on making that new behavior a part of every moment in the kitchen. Gradually you can add other elements borrowed from any worthwhile source, including your own imagination.

ON THE HORIZON

Ask the person whose kitchen presence you admire to dinner. Prepare a meal for him in a calm and attentive manner. Telling him why he has been invited is not necessary, though it may happen. For example, Adam Gopnik has written of a meal he prepared for Alice Waters when she was visiting Paris. His *New Yorker* article describes nervous days and nights planning, shopping for, and cooking a three-course meal. Gopnik is closely tied to the result of his cooking, which he finds wanting, a likely result given that an inspired culinary presence is the guest of honor and inevitable taster, but he thoroughly enjoys the social experience of the meal.

FORMAL TOFU • *Serves 4*

One of my cooking partners in Berkeley was Fu Tung Cheng, then a Tai Chi instructor, now a celebrated designer of kitchens. For Fu Tung, life is filled with opportunities to laugh. Almost any situation, no matter how dire, can provide the impetus for a joke. There is a bit of the slyly subversive Buddhist monk in this man. It was his ability to turn a dark culinary moment into an occasion for side-splitting mirth that helped me put into perspective my achievement mania. As a way of marking my independence from elaborate, banquet-style cooking and expressing appreciation for his approach to the kitchen, I invited him to a "formal dinner." The table was covered with linen; candles provided a soothing glow. I had borrowed a waiter's outfit complete with bow tie and matching black apron. I refused to answer any questions about the menu, preferring to let him speculate about the reasons for the secrecy. The food was brought to the table in silver serving dishes. With a flourish I lifted the lids and, *voilà,* formal tofu and brown rice.

· · · · · · · · · · · · · · · · · · · ·

2 tablespoons peanut or canola oil

1 tablespoon grated ginger

1 tablespoon chopped garlic

1 dried red chili, ground

1 tablespoon soy sauce

2 tablespoons sesame paste or peanut butter

2 tablespoons red or brown miso
 mixed with ½ cup water

1 teaspoon honey

1 pound firm tofu, cut into ¾-inch cubes

1 teaspoon cornstarch dissolved in
 2 tablespoons of water

2 scallions, minced

1 teaspoon sesame oil

Heat the peanut oil in a wok or large frying pan. Add the ginger, garlic, and red chili, and cook over medium heat for 1 minute. Combine the soy sauce, sesame paste, miso, and honey in a bowl. Add the tofu to the pan. Cook for a few seconds. Add the soy sauce mixture. Lower the heat and simmer for 5 minutes. Add the dissolved cornstarch and stir until the sauce thickens. Serve over brown rice garnished with the scallions. Top with the sesame oil. Think of the irrepressible Fu Tung as you enjoy it.

CHAPTER TWO

A SPIRITUAL
JOURNEY
THROUGH THE
HISTORY
OF FOOD

*So long as cooks kept their knowledge to
themselves and only recipes were made public, the results of such labors were simply the
products of art (and religion we might add).
But then at last, perhaps too late, men of science came upon the scene. They examined,
analyzed and classified all foodstuffs, and reduced them to their basic elements. They
plumbed the mysteries of assimilation, followed inert matter through all its metamor-
phoses, and saw how it might come to life.*

—JEAN-ANTHELME BRILLAT-SAVARIN,
THE PHYSIOLOGY OF TASTE

At the end of the movie *Little Big Man,* the old Lakota chief believes that his time has come to die. With Dustin Hoffman, as the character Jack Crabb, standing mournfully beside him, the chief lies down on the ground and sings the ancient death chant of his tribe, calling upon the divine spirit to take him from this world and transport him to whatever comes next.

At last the aged warrior falls silent. He's lying motionless. His eyes are closed. Hoffman just stands there.

Suddenly the chief opens his eyes. "Am I dead?" he asks.

"I don't think so," Hoffman replies.

The chief sighs and slowly gets to his feet. "Well, sometimes the magic works," he says, "and sometimes it doesn't."

Indeed, that may be an important difference between magic and science. Science has to work every time. If the results of an experiment you did this morning can't be duplicated this afternoon, or can't be duplicated next week by someone else a thousand miles away, then those results must be considered invalid.

Today most people approach cooking from a scientific point of view. Recipes are almost identical to laboratory protocols, which have been tested time and again and have been found to deliver predictable results. If you follow the recipe carefully, the dish will turn out as you desire and expect. If it doesn't, you must have done something wrong.

This is the way most people cook, and I suppose to a great extent it is the "right" way. Let me contrast it, however, with a friend of mine who makes the most wonderful red spaghetti sauce. Because Jack is a magician in the kitchen, rather than a scientist, he cooks intuitively rather than perceptively. Jack doesn't use exactly the same ingredients every time, and he doesn't work with a written recipe, so he doesn't have a precise idea of how much parsley or basil he uses in the sauce. If you call him on the phone and ask for his recipe, he won't really be able to give it to you in a traditional form. To learn how to make his sauce, you have to watch him and take notes.

Obviously, Jack is not what most people would call a "serious cook." He's much more like a shaman or priest: someone with a particular kind of power. For invited guests he doesn't attempt many dishes other than spaghetti, but on a good day he serves the very best bolognese around.

When a member of the Lakota tribe had a frightening or dangerous experience—if he heard an owl calling, for example—he would seek out someone with "owl power" to help solve the problem. Jack has spaghetti sauce power.

In this chapter we'll trace the transformation of cooking from a spiritual to an essentially scientific enterprise. We'll see how food lost its fundamental religious component and became amenable to the methods of modern science. And we'll consider how, in this journey from holy element to experimental data, food and cooking have lost the ritual power to unify a community and have become another subject of reductionist investigation—just another fragment among many broken pieces.

BIBLICAL AND JEWISH TRADITIONS

Food, the preparation of food, and eating are important motifs in the Bible, and from the very beginning these subjects are shrouded in mystery. Why are Adam and Eve forbidden to eat the fruit of only two trees? Why does God reject the vegetable sacrifice offered to him by Cain, while accepting Abel's slaughtered animals? Perhaps most significantly, what is the basis of the complex dietary laws and restrictions set forth in the Bible and the Talmud, which to this day are a unifying feature of the lives of observant Jews in all parts of the world?

In fact, traditional Judaism makes no attempt to offer a rational basis for the dietary laws. The laws are simply presented as an element of a righteous and holy life (Leviticus 11:44). From an Orthodox point of view, the idea that prohibiting pork was intended to prevent trichinosis is an offensive rationalization. An observant Jew shuns pork because God says not to eat pork. A kosher butcher slaughters an animal with a knife twice as thick as the animal's throat because that's the kind of knife the sacred writings prescribe.

Looked at from the outside, however, it seems clear that the dietary laws have an exclusionist aspect, separating Jew from non-Jew in a fundamental way. Because "keeping kosher" requires strict separation of dairy from meat products, an observant household must have at least two complete sets of dishes. Ideally, there will also be two sinks and separate counter space for the two food categories. If dairy and meat inadvertently come into contact, there are procedures for reestablishing the kosher kitchen.

Keeping a kosher house presents many practical difficulties, but it also endows cooking with a profound spiritual significance. Food is understood as a gift from God, and preparing food is an expression of God's wisdom. The prayers and blessings that attend each meal are testimony to this.

EARLY CHRISTIANITY

Throughout the New Testament, Jesus describes adherence to God's will as an internal condition of love and acceptance, rather than adherence to laws and prohibitions. Christianity, therefore, does not exclude certain foods or ways of preparing them. Although for a portion of its history the Catholic church forbade the eating of meat on Fridays, this has now been rescinded (except during the season of Lent).

Yet the preparing of food is perhaps more central to Christianity than to any other major religion. For the Catholic and Anglican denominations, the sacrament of the Mass is built around the transformation of bread and wine into the Eucharist, the body and blood of Jesus Christ. This ceremony, of course, is derived from Christ's celebration of the Jewish feast of Passover, popularly called the Last Supper, which is described in the New Testament.

In the early years of Christianity, breaking bread and drinking in a spirit of gratitude and piety was part of every meal shared by the faithful. Later, in the ceremony of Communion, the fervent sharing of food and drink became ritualized in the Mass. It remains part of daily life through the saying of grace over meals.

THE VEDIC KITCHEN

Perhaps more than any other tradition, Indian cooking emphasizes the importance of intention and emotion. In the West we believe that good cooking depends first of all on good ingredients; it seems almost heretical to believe that a cheeseburger and an order of french fries could be anything but an unhealthy experience. From a traditional Indian perspective, however, a hamburger can be the healthiest food in the world if it's prepared and served in a spirit of affection and good will.

The Bhagavad Gita, one of the sacred texts of Indian literature, teaches that the consciousness of the cook is transferred to his or her food. A loving cook strengthens the healing powers of a dish, while an agitated or unhappy cook creates food that is far less nourishing. Therefore, the essence of cooking resides not in the chemically measured nutritional qualities of the ingredients, but in the dynamic, transformational powers of the cook. To paraphrase Deepak Chopra, a respect for the wonder of transformation inherent in food leads us to regard every meal as a celebration.

For the Vedic chef, cooking embodies the continuing opportunity to experience three spiritual moments: attention, ritual, and focus or perspective. Foods are divided into categories according to how they look and taste. They correspond to personality types. Vata combines air and space. The vata foods are blue or green in color. Pitta is water and earth, which correspond to blue and green. Kapha is water and earth, and is embodied in red and orange ingredients. Much of Vedic medicine involves the balancing of these food groups and the positive preparation of food.

Spicy foods are important not simply because they are flavorful. Piquant flavors correspond to the life force because they contain and produce energy. Chopra feels that the fresher food is, the more of the life force it contains, and who can argue with him? The Vedic kitchen seeks to enhance the unity of cooking, the cook and the food.

THE EUROPEAN TRADITIONS

Throughout the centuries, the preparation and content of meals for the common people has been determined by the constraints of realism rather than the possibilities of ceremony. Under the feudal system that came into being after the fall of Rome, small farmers worked land owned by the nobility, and in return were allowed to keep a portion of the harvest. Individual families could also raise pigs, cows, or chickens, assuming they were willing to live in very close contact with these barnyard animals. But despite the very limited culinary opportunities available to most people, the Middle Ages was also a period in which a rich and complex institution of banquets developed among the aristocracy. While this drew heavily upon the Roman tradition, a religious association was added, so that the greatest feasts were occasioned by holidays such as Christmas and Easter.

These banquets were sensual experiences in the broadest terms. Music, for example, was scrupulously planned for dramatic effect. Permanent court performers or those invited for special occasions followed a musical menu as carefully crafted as the culinary one. The number of instruments, the blending of their sounds, appositions among lyrics of songs, alternations between solo and choral settings—all these existed in delicate balance with the feast's many courses.

The meal itself was an artful succession of foods in time. So abundant were the exotic foods that it was often difficult to find places for the silver platters before the diners. Two guests shared as many as twelve dishes between them, plus beer and wine. Whatever could be wished for should be available. Just as God's creation of the world expressed His unlimited powers and infinite variety, the banquet was intended to mirror the Creator's bounty. The abundance of food on the table should be no less than the abundance that set sail on Noah's ark.

With the ascendancy of rationalism and commerce during the Enlightenment, the religious element in the preparation and service of food was replaced by secular regulations and market forces. This was especially true as the institution of the commercial restaurant came into being during and after the French Revolution.

These new governing principles, however, were no less numerous and detailed. In England, codfish caught west of London Bridge were to be sold only near the Conduit after 10 A.M., while shellfish could not be offered at shops but were to be peddled through the streets and lanes by itinerant hawkers only. Red and white wines from France were not to be sold in the same taverns as sweet wines from Crete. Specific weights and measures bore official seals and insignias guaranteeing standards, and prices were scrupulously monitored. Various types of bread could be sold for no more than established prices for specific weights, and distinctions were made between light breads and dark. The pillory was the usual punishment for conviction of bread fraud, and a baker thrice convicted was forced to forswear trade in London forever.

PRECOLONIAL AMERICA

The Native American tribes of New England were sophisticated and resourceful farmers, despite the fact that they had no working animals. Their diets were generally diverse and imaginative, including beans, corn, and squash along with fish and game. As an early European settler described it, "Every food whether plant or animal is considered sacred, and the acts of hunting, growing, gathering, cooking and eating take on a spiritual aspect akin to prayer." The most sacred of all Native American foods was corn. Most prized were the yellow, blue, red, white, multicolored, and black varieties, in that order, which symbolized the six cardinal directions—north, west, south, east, up, and down. Thus, corn defined secular and religious time and space in the lives of Native Americans. According to Waverley Root, "In the West corn dances were performed during the growing season to persuade good spirits to grant a bountiful crop or even to withhold their malevolence. Corn was considered to have miraculous powers. The Zuni would sprinkle it across their gateways to keep the conquistadors out."

BRILLAT-SAVARIN AND THE
RISE OF FOOD SCIENCE

A great deal of what we perceive as a modern approach to food originates in the writings of Jean-Anthelme Brillat-Savarin, particularly *The Physiology of Taste,* published in 1825. This work was one of the crowning achievements of the rationalism and materialism that were at the foundation of French thought. Just as René Descartes created a school of philosophy that separated mind and body so that each could be studied separately, Brillat-Savarin sought to understand food as an interdisciplinary science—gastronomy—that included natural history, physics, and chemistry. At the same time, Brillat-Savarin saw the huge social significance of the well-thought-out and well-executed meal. Almost single-handedly he championed the notion of the banquet as political force. "Meals," he wrote, "have become a means of government, and the fate of nations has often been sealed at a banquet." Perhaps this is the origin of the anxiety felt by so many modern cooks. After all, if a properly prepared dinner of state can influence world affairs, perhaps our own personal histories depend on perfectly turned-out meals.

THE RISE OF MANUFACTURED FOOD

At the same time that Brillat-Savarin was publishing his philosophical insights into cooking and food, important practical innovations were taking place on the other side of the Atlantic. Thomas Kensett received the first patent for a tin can in 1825, and in 1856 Gail Borden was awarded a patent for concentrated milk, a substance that was quickly tinned. By 1875 Gustavus Swift and Philip Armour had brought refrigeration to the railroad industry; ice was gathered from frozen lakes during the winter and stored in insulated buildings for the rest of the year. Swift and Armour also introduced technology that would allow the efficient unloading of whole carcasses weighing hundreds of pounds directly into cold storage units.

Container innovations centered around breakfast cereals. Post and Kellogg produced products whose sales depended upon packaging, since the content itself was not a breakthrough. The changes in the packaging industry that came rapidly after the turn of the century were largely a result of financial concerns. Packaging reduced losses from damage and spoilage. This was its primary purpose, rather than the prevention of disease, as the industry claimed. And there were other benefits for the food industry. With products encased in cardboard, waxed paper, or tin, buyers could no longer see, touch, and smell what they were getting. According to the food historian Waverley Root, the period of great American home cooking occurred between 1812 and 1861, when there was enough time and resources to devote to the preparation of locally produced ingredients, which existed in abundance and great variety. The preserving of foods for sale outside the local region inevitably led to a decline in quality and a reduction of choice. The Civil War accelerated the development of processed foods because huge armies had to be fed day after day. Individual households could now purchase labor-saving prepared foods rather than use fresh ingredients grown or slaughtered at home or by nearby artisans.

Today the subcultures that keep alive the frontier tradition of self-sufficiency and that celebrate the virtues of homemade foods are, not surprisingly, religious orders such as the Mennonites. These farming communities devote themselves almost entirely to a religious and aesthetic pursuit of life's simple necessities: food, clothing, and shelter. Like the Native Americans, they see food as God's gift, a gift they must work very hard to harvest and to deserve.

AMERICA TODAY: FOOD AS APPEARANCE

"Americans seem heavily committed to the extraneous aspects of eating—color, drama, showmanship, and the need for something to talk about. Such factors at the best contribute nothing to the intrinsic quality of food; usually they are at war with it." Waverley Root's pessimistic appraisal, written in 1974, would seem to be confirmed by current trends in American cooking. Despite the fact that a resurgent small family farming movement has created opportunities for many city dwellers to avail themselves of fresh, seasonal produce and other foods, despite the growth of ethnic foods distribution networks, and despite the appearance of hundreds of restaurants and markets offering high-quality foods based on these ingredients, the majority of Americans do not avail themselves of these possibilities. They frequently choose food that looks good but lacks real flavor.

At both ends of the income ladder, we seem concerned

with what food says about us. It may be, "I can afford the most exotic and expensive ingredients, arranged like a work of art" or "I am so busy that meals are just fuel to take me somewhere more interesting." We base our diets on appearances, whether of the food itself or the nutritional information on the package. We judge our diets by the look of what is put in front of us, supplemented, in the case of purchased ingredients, by a nutritional analysis that lists everything except one key component—the emotional/spiritual content of the food. Food acquires a spiritual connotation only in the context of a few religious holidays such as Easter, Passover, Christmas, Ramadan, the Chinese New Year, and the secular ritual of Thanksgiving.

More than two thousand years ago, the Greek philosopher Heraclitus developed the idea that the world is constantly changing. "Upon those who step into the same rivers different and ever different waters flow down," Heraclitus supposedly declared, though this idea is often more simply expressed as, "You can't step into the same river twice." The notion that the universe is in constant flux has many applications to cooking, for in truth you can't step into the same kitchen twice. You can't slice the same tomato, and therefore you can't make the same meal. You can't even cook for the same people, even if you're cooking only for yourself. Perhaps you made a peanut butter sandwich for your child yesterday, but that child is gone. Among other things, the child who's waiting now for a sandwich is a day older—and so is the peanut butter, the bread, and yourself.

This holistic approach to cooking, based on the idea that

all the variables are important, is at odds with what might be called a scientific approach to cooking. If so, I'm quite pleased—because as you'll see throughout this book, there's much to be learned and enjoyed even when the "magic" doesn't work. Like other spiritual practices, good cooking is a journey rather than a destination.

A MINDFUL LOOK: YOUR FOOD PAST

We all have food histories, changing relationships to food, to what, where, and how we eat. These histories largely determine our current approach to food much as the social history just recounted determines larger attitudes. Reviewing our personal food pasts will support us in the process of becoming more mindful in the present moment.

1. What were your parents' attitudes toward food?
2. How and when were meals served during your childhood?
3. What kind of preparation time and technique was involved?
4. Who did the cooking?
5. What foods were emphasized?
6. What kinds of ingredients were used? Where did they come from?
7. What was the mood at family meals?
8. How much time was spent around the dinner table?
9. Did either of your parents teach you how to cook?

10. What region of the country did you grow up in? How did regional tastes influence what you ate?

11. Was your family's diet different from the national trend?

12. As you move toward the present, pose the same kinds of questions for the various stages of your life. Do you notice trends or changes?

13. Do these changes move you toward or away from mindful cooking?

A MINDFUL STEP: A FOOD DIARY

Keep a food diary for a week. Record everything that you ate and that you wanted to eat. You be may be drawn by a spectacular-looking raw ingredient or a prepared dish in a shop window, see something in a magazine, or crave something on a restaurant menu. This is not a weight-watching exercise. Don't concern yourself with calories or nutrients or moral judgments. Don't censor yourself. Try to put into words what is appealing about each of these foods.

ON THE HORIZON

Create a visual food chart that presents foods according to your own personally experienced and preferred categories. Forget about the standard food groups; invent your own. Diagram the interrelationships, hierarchies, complementary compatibilities, incompatibilities, and so on. Try to graphically incorporate the influences on your development as well. You may want to do several of these to trace your culinary development over the stages of your life. A personal food time line would be another way to deepen your understanding of this history.

My family's approach to eating changed in a way that followed the typical American pattern of assimilation. Gradually ethnic dishes such as gefilte fish, matzoh-ball soup, and pot roast were replaced with steak and hamburgers from the barbecue and fried chicken. A few of the Eastern European–style favorites remained in the repertoire. Among them is this rich-tasting potato dish.

DIANE'S POTATO BAKE • *Serves 4*

This recipe was given to me by my sister. It was originally written out longhand by my mother on a three-by-five-inch card along with gefilte fish, stewed brisket, and matzoh-ball soup. I remember the nutty smell of the potatoes and garlic filling the kitchen on winter nights. As a family we often had meat as a main course. Somehow this dish seemed more satisfying.

. . . .

4 large russet potatoes

2 tablespoons butter

2 tablespoons olive oil

4 cloves garlic, chopped

1 tablespoon chopped fresh thyme

Salt to taste

Scrub the potatoes and cut them into ¼-inch slices, leaving the skin on. In a large sauté pan or skillet, melt the butter and add the olive oil. Sauté the garlic in the oil and butter over medium heat for 1 minute. Take off the heat. Toss the potatoes in the pan until the slices are evenly coated. Transfer to a baking dish. Top with the thyme and salt. Bake at 400 degrees for 25 minutes. Turn up the heat to broil. Move the dish close to the flame and brown the top.

TOMATO - GARLIC - BASIL PARAL

45° North   UNITED STATES

                             HEIRLOOM TOMATO S

MEAT AND FRUIT PARALLEL

30° North   MEXICO

                             CHICKEN WITH
                             MANGO GUACAMOLE

CILANTRO - JALAPEÑO - GARLIC PARAL

15° North

ITALY

BRUSCHETTA

OCCO   IRAN

B AND PRUNES
ON-OLIVE CHICKEN

                        DUCK WITH POMEGRANATE
                        AND WALNUT

N   THAI
RIED SPLIT PEAS   SPICY TOFU

CHAPTER THREE

THE
MINDFUL
KITCHEN

The kitchen is the true center of a home, the focal point of our domestic lives, the real "living room." As such it accurately reflects our approach to experience in general and to preparing and serving food in particular. The kitchen is the room we ran to as children, and it is the place we remember as adults. It is where the fishbowl sat on the windowsill and the dog's bowl stood in the corner. It was the source of nourishment and the wellspring of love, and it still is—or should be.

In contemporary kitchen design the central organizing principle is the work triangle, the three points of which are the cooktop, the sink, and the refrigerator. Creating or refining a kitchen space is structured by the physical relationship among these functions.

The mindful kitchen has its own triangle that embodies three essential elements of mindful cooking—attention, openness to change, and memory. They relate directly to the points of the work triangle. These elements are reminiscent of the division of the zodiac—fire, air, water, and earth, with earth ever present as the foundation of everything in the kitchen.

The value of each of these elements can be seen most clearly in kitchens where imbalance reigns. The kamikaze kitchen has an overemphasis on change. The controlled kitchen is dominated by attention. The survival kitchen places too great a weight on the power of memory.

THE KAMIKAZE KITCHEN

The kamikaze kitchen is strong on openness to change, wedded to attention in an impossible dance, and very short on memory. It is a wet, hot place with never enough space. I should know. I was a kamikaze cook in an out-of-control kitchen, one of the bold culinary risk takers in a town known for its risk takers. My small cooking space with its standard four-burner gas stove, tiny dishwasher, moderate refrigerator, and single stainless sink with limited counter space and storage was conceived as a space for a family of three to prepare simple meals. It was not intended for the purpose I subjected it to: catering.

The most elaborate job I took on was brought to me by none other than Fu Tung, the subversive Buddhist. Fu, ever the generous spirit, had decided to give a Christmas party for the entire Tai Chi Dojo (the teaching studio) and their families and friends, some seventy people. His kitchen was in a shambles, part of a never-ending remodel, so we decided to cook in mine. We finally settled on seven or so courses, the *pièce de résistance* being Beijing duck, a dish neither of us had made before. By the time the ingredients were fully assembled the supplies extended halfway across the living room, with produce, bags of rice, and pots and pans scattered in random disarray. After each dish was completed we had to rearrange the mess, freeing up counter space and juggling cookware and refrigerator space, expanded by ice chests, in an elaborate dance. Finished dishes were piled nearly up to the ceiling.

On the end of the second full day of cooking we got around to the Beijing duck. Traditionally, the duck is roasted whole hanging on a hook in a large oven, with the skin partially separated from the meat so that it becomes extra crisp while cooking. The meat is then cut into bite-size pieces, while the skin is served separately along with moo shoo pancakes and sweet plum dipping sauce.

Our recipe called for the use of a bicycle pump to blow air between the skin and meat. Well, why not? But it wasn't that simple. Though we had pumped up tires and basketballs, we had never pumped a duck, and too much pressure caused the skin to tear in a number of places. An elaborate plastic surgery was attempted in which I "grafted" skin from the underside to more visible areas on top of the bird. After the operation, our duck looked like Frankenstein the Fowl, but we had hopes the patient would still be ambulatory. Sadly, most of the grafts tore, negating many hours of effort. I wasn't sure whether to laugh or cry, so I did a lot of both! This is not an atypical result for the out-of-balance kamikaze kitchen.

THE CONTROLLED KITCHEN

The controlled kitchen is, in many ways, the polar opposite of the kamikaze. *Attention and memory reign to a fault. Openness to change is almost nowhere to be found.* Everything is orderly and focused, not unlike a military regiment on the march. Things repeat themselves in predictable patterns. The burners are part of a tightly orchestrated strategy. It is almost as if the metamorphosis inherent in cooking is a constant threat. Not a drop of liquid is allowed to remain unmopped, let alone a spilled ingredient. If events fall out from the original battle plan, watch out. The controlled kitchen is cool, too cool.

Take the kitchen of a friend of mine. Guy is a wonderful cook and a good friend. In our case, dissimilars attract. His approach is at the opposite end of the spectrum to my kamikaze-like personality. Guy is organized—in everything. In his office he saves his computer files every day on no less than three tape backups that he constantly rotates. If you want to see his check register from 1986, just ask him for it. When he bakes, which he does often and masterfully, everything is measured with a metric scale down to the nearest gram. Assuming that everything proceeds according to a prearranged plan, there is no problem—that is, as long as you have a lot of time on your hands. Being so perfectly accurate is frequently an involved process complete with checking and double checking. If a mistake occurs, Guy simply begins again. Dinner—which is, let us say, supposed to be served at eight—sometimes shows up after ten thirty.

Recently Guy volunteered to make an apple tart for a holiday dinner. When I told him the guest list had grown to the point that one tart would not be enough, he froze. He had only one deep copper mold that was required for the tart tatin he had decided to make. My first reaction to his response was disbelief. I'll buy a chocolate cake, I thought. Recovering my composure I suggested that he make a second fruit dessert following a different recipe using a traditional tart mold, a concept that Guy would probably not easily have come up with on his own. He liked the idea. Calm had been restored. The minicrisis had passed.

THE SURVIVAL KITCHEN

The survival kitchen is a kitchen by default. What goes on there is something like a Taylorized nutrition factory with every step measured in terms of time saved and energy conserved. Even counting calories is an extension of seeing the body as a machine. Unfortunately, the survival kitchen is all too prevalent across America, particularly in families with young children.

In the survival kitchen memory in the form of repetition is dominant. The refrigerator and the freezer are the focus of cooking because preprepared and/or microwavable food is a key building block. Dishes are selected from a small list of standards. *Attention and openness to change are almost nonexistent.* They would only slow down the food conveyor belt. The usual kitchen tools are not generally in evidence. They have been rendered obsolete.

We have seen the survival kitchen in nearly every commercial. Typically a hurried breakfast is in progress. Cereal is being consumed by one kid as another grabs a now heated, previously frozen waffle from the toaster and slops syrup on it as he gets up from the table. Mom eats hastily out of a yogurt container. Dad runs through the kitchen passing out dabs of affection and grabs a cup of coffee for the road. He says he will be late for dinner. Who cares? Dinner will unfold over several hours as different family members return home, microwave their entrées, and go about their evening routines without ever meeting over a meal.

What each of these kitchens have in common is that they are out of balance. One of the three key elements, one corner of the mindful triangle, is dominant. There is a sense of artificiality at best and of fear at worst. These kitchens are self-fulfilling prophecies because they systematically exclude what would make them different. In the kamikaze kitchen a sense of proportion and planning that would have been seen as unadventurous would have precluded attempting the Beijing duck. Experimentation that would break the controlled kitchen out of its rut introduces a level of uncertainty that could result in an unpredictable result, or even a failure, the one thing that cannot be tolerated. Focusing closely on food could never happen in the survival kitchen; it might subvert the entire day that is planned around making a routine out of everything.

THE MINDFUL KITCHEN

How does a mindful kitchen differ from one that is not mindful? The first words that come to mind are *balance and har-*

mony. Unlike the kamikaze, the controlling, and the survival environments, where a single note is being played over and over again, no one element—attention, memory, or change—predominates. The cook is at home and in firm control without a sense that an ego is simply being served. Anything is permitted and yet there is a respect for tradition, that whatever is new will not be simply innovation for the sake of change, that it will come from real feeling. Surprise and continuity walk hand in hand. The simplest things are attended to with as much care as the final presentation. There is a sense of passion without compulsion, in other words, of freedom.

Being in the mindful kitchen is a soothing experience for others. This is not the case with any of the unbalanced kitchens we have described. Guests are as welcome in the kitchen as at the dining-room table because the mindful kitchen is not a place of secretiveness, misplaced insecurity, or perfectionism.

The mindful kitchen is distinguished by its outlook. There are a few simple details that if attended to will go a long way toward creating a balanced kitchen. Tools are important, mainly when they serve as a limitation to mindful cooking. Dull knives, for example, prevent us from focusing on the experience because we are concerned about how much effort a simple chopping task takes or, worse still, whether the knife will rebound and cut us. Thin cookware with poorly insulated handles make extra work because the items are harder to control, require more heat and more manipulation, and create a sense of dread based on the possibility of being burned. The lack of basic tools (a long-bladed spatula, a pair of spring-loaded tongs, a sharp vegetable peeler, a slotted spoon, a colander, a wire whisk, a ladle, wooden spoons for stirring, a rubber scraper, a pasta fork, an adequate number of mixing bowls), burners that don't light on their own, poor illumination—all can contribute to a sense of unease that takes us far away from the essential.

A MINDFUL LOOK

Obviously the three types—kamikaze, controlling, and survival—are somewhat extreme. You will probably not fit neatly into any of these categories. Take a look at yourself and your kitchen through these questions.

1. How much time do you spend in the kitchen each day?
2. What part of the kitchen do you find yourself in most often? What are you doing there?
3. What kitchen activity do you most enjoy? What do you avoid?
4. What kind of mood most often characterizes your time in the kitchen?
5. How would you describe your kitchen ambience? Which of these types is it closest to? Why?
6. Describe a kitchen you have seen that you would enjoy being in. How is it different from yours?
7. If you could change one thing about your kitchen, what would it be?

8. If you could completely remodel your kitchen, how would it look?

9. What, if anything, would you do differently in this fantasy space?

A   M I N D F U L   S T E P :   A   F I E L D   T R I P

A field trip is a good way to break out of routine. As school kids we welcomed them like no other activity. Many of my most exhilarating food experiences have come from eating in restaurants where it is possible to observe the chef as he or she works. Restaurants increasingly display some part of their kitchens as entertainment. Of course the charm of the traditional lunch counter is based on the close proximity between the cook and the patrons.

This exercise is one of pure observation. Pay a visit to a restaurant you like that has some substantial portion of its cooking operation fully visible. The layout and pace will obviously be different because of the demands of fast-moving, large-scale production. Order something different from the menu than your typical choice or choices just to set the mood.

Now observe everything that the cook does in interacting with the kitchen space. Take a look at how the space is laid out, how the various functions are coordinated, how the physical elements of the work triangle relate to each other, which is emphasized. Can you see how they interact with the mindful triangle of elements and with the end product, the finished plate? Are the balance of elements reflected in the conception you had of the restaurant?

ON THE HORIZON

Transport that cooking style to your home kitchen. Ideally, this approach will be as different from your own style as possible. Make a meal using the observed cook's approach to the elements of the work triangle. This is not an imitation, but more like an acting exercise. You may want to use ingredients or a recipe or even a way of holding a sauté pan or a style of slicing inspired by the restaurant and its chef as a starting point.

FENNEL SALAD À LA FRANK • *Serves 4*

I believe I am drawn to Frank, a lively, packed-like-sardines Italian restaurant located in New York's hip Lower East Side because it reminds me of a controlled version of my own kamikaze kitchen. Balance is achieved by elaborate and thorough preparation, and a calm at the center of the storm in the person of the unflappable Frank that allows the headlong dash to stay on track. The cooking area is totally open and I choose to sit on a stool at the counter, feel the heat from the six burners, and watch Frank work the stovetop. The work space is very small, and things inevitably spill in the dance that is required to turn out meals for the fast-turning tables (on a weekend night Frank serves an astonishing 140 people in a restaurant that seats twenty-eight). The three points of the triangle are so close together everything must be in balance. I get the sense that I am part of a mad scientist's experiment that somehow always turns out. The food choices reflect the same sense of freedom, offering unusual ingredients for such a limited menu.

Fennel Salad, as befits the impromptu nature of the kamikaze kitchen, is made to order for each person who requests it and served within seconds of being completed.

• •

> 2 bulbs fresh fennel, green leaves removed
> 1 cup extra virgin olive oil
> ¼ cup balsamic vinegar
> 2 teaspoons finely grated, high-quality Italian
>   Parmesan cheese
> Salt and pepper to taste

Slice the fennel very fine crosswise using a meat slicer on the smallest setting or with the thinnest slicing disk for the food processor. Try to make the slices paper thin, almost translucent. Make a dressing with the oil and vinegar. Toss your desired amount of dressing with the fennel. Top with the cheese, salt, and pepper. Serve immediately.

CHAPTER FOUR

MINDFUL SELECTION

> When you eat something you should chew it
> carefully and slowly. When you sense the
> sourness, sweetness, bitterness and pungency
> then you know the flavor. When you know the
> flavor you eat what tastes good and reject
> what tastes bad. . . . When you are done with
> one level, then you enter another level, finish-
> ing with one after another, entering one after
> another, until there is no more to enter into,
> and you'll see what is underneath it all recog-
> nizing the ultimate source. Only then have
> you realized the ultimate accomplishment.
> This is like tasting food before eating it.
>
> **—LIU I-MING, *AWAKENING TO THE TAO***

I have a confession to make, and perhaps a surprising one coming from a person who loves to cook. It's not that I don't enjoy being in the kitchen; I do. But I love shopping at the farmer's market more, and even more pleasurable than being in the market is being in the fields where food is grown. Here I can experience the essence of raw ingredients. In the field there is nothing to distract me, no other ingredients, no cookbooks, no kitchen tools. Once I sense what it is, feel what it is, appreciate what it is, the picking, washing, and kitchen preparation take place instantaneously in my mind and my heart. In short, seeing is tasting. I believe this is what Liu I-Ming means when he says, "This is like tasting food before eating it."

In a similar way, when I go to the farmer's market I do my shopping not by looking first at the food, but by looking at the farmer. My perception of him or her always comes first and frequently obviates any need for evaluating the wares spread out on the table. If I am on the fence I look at the overall feel and mood of the stall. Is it orderly and attractive, untidy or even chaotic? Finally I consider the food itself. It's easy to produce a bright red, beautiful, but tasteless tomato. Appearances can be deceiving. I'm convinced that I can sense the pride, the joy, and even the quality of attention that a farmer feels toward his or her product. This may not qualify as a true sixth sense, but it has always led me to delicious ingredients. I've learned to trust my instincts and to respect this silent form of communication, and as you become a Mindful Cook you'll find yourself doing likewise.

Maybe my sense of identification with the producer's

commitment to his or her products and the possibility of discerning that approach comes from my own experience. For several years I helped a small company called Kenter Canyon Farms grow and market organic salad lettuces in southern California. We worked closely with the chefs who were our customers to develop products tailored to their needs (this was before the farmer's market movement had reached Los Angeles, and our only business was wholesale), while creating plate-ready foods in the garden. Many of the chefs would visit us to see what the plants looked like as they grew. They would harvest a few leaves and taste them in the field at the moment of prime freshness. A vital exchange would take place as the cooks would make suggestions and gather information at the same time.

Each day we would produce the various salad mixes by hand-tossing several hundred pounds of salad greens. Our approach was to make the mix each day with what was at its peak that morning while maintaining certain parameters of taste and beauty. I loved making the mix because I was always surprised at how stunning the salad looked with its variety of colors and shapes. I felt that this literally hands-on approach to salad could be experienced by those who ate our greens. Of course our organic farming methods and delivering the salad a few hours after cutting it didn't hurt either, but in a way they were also part of our commitment, our sense of urgency, and our respect for nature's bounty.

As a Mindful Cook you can experience the correlation between the attention of the farmer and the taste and look of food in a number of ways.

1. Most obviously, you can become that farmer yourself by creating a garden in your backyard or even in a small terrace space.

2. You can visit family farmers in your region, many of whom would welcome your interest. For example, Fairview Gardens Farm in Goleta, north of Santa Barbara, offers a self-guided tour of its seventeen acres. Farmers are available to answer questions, and the day's pick is on sale at the roadside stand. Closer to home, in more ways than one, on the very day that I was working on this section of the book, perhaps even at the same hour in the afternoon, a friend of mine, Trish Marx, was driving on Highway 8 by the Good Shepherd's Farm three-quarters of a mile south of Masonville, New York. Kyle Smith's three and a half acres of organic produce surrounds his store on three sides. Trish pulled up and began speaking to Kyle. He related the history of the farm and his philosophy in cheerful detail. When he offered spinach, chard, broccoli, and other items not on the stand, she assumed that he would retrieve them from a storage area. He returned with bags brimming with vegetables, explaining that he had gone into the field and cut her produce "to order." This is the way things work at the Good Shepherd's Farm. Anything that is particularly perishable—squash, radishes, Swiss chard, spinach, cucumbers, collards, broccoli, cauliflower—is harvested at that moment. Smith welcomes visitors and offers informal tours, time permitting.

3. You can participate in the harvesting process yourself by visiting U-pick plots where you are welcome to gather berries, apples, or other produce.

4. You can attend harvest festivals in rural areas near you. Generally these events are held in the summer months. There are countless celebrations around the country commemorating crops of garlic, artichokes, blueberries, chili peppers, potatoes, and so on. Chez Panisse takes this one step further. Each summer it honors all its farmers who supply the restaurant's organic produce with a dinner featuring their fruits and vegetables. The restaurant's patrons interact directly with the growers as they share a meal.

5. And you can visit your local farmer's market if you live in or near any major metropolitan center in the United States.

A MINDFUL LOOK

This set of questions will help you focus on your own approach to buying foods. You can answer by "taking" the queries with you on your next visit to the store or market, or better, by recalling recent shopping trips.

1. When you go to buy produce or other fresh foods, what is your buying style and your organizing principle(s)? Are you totally list-driven, predominantly impulsive, or do you make choices based on a cooking philosophy such as low-fat or vegetarian?

2. What patterns or habits determine your selections? For example, do you walk through one portion of the market first, allowing that to determine future choices?

3. How frequently do you allow yourself to be swayed away from your lists and plans by encounters with the unexpected?

4. How often does food shopping determine your day's plans as a focus? Or is it always an adjunct to other activities?

5. Are you always in a hurry when you shop?

NAVIGATING THE MARKET

The essence of the act of selection is having meaningful criteria to reduce a broad range of choices to a manageable few. Knowing what you are choosing therefore also means knowing what you have not chosen. A Mindful Cook learns not only to understand what he or she wants and needs but also the nature of what is not useful, what is not selected. This is not a negative act; it is part of having a whole view. We can understand more about what pleases us by looking at what does not.

That is why I begin every trip to the farmer's market (or the grocery store) with a tour of all the produce. I look at perfect tomatoes and lettuces, but I also make a point of noticing the ones that fail to attain the same level of charisma, that do not radiate pride. My walk through the market or the produce section completed one time, I buy on the way back.

1. Though I have certain things in mind, based mostly on the season, I allow myself to be literally drawn to what is special or unusual the way you would to an unknown but interesting-looking individual at a social gathering. I have found that going with a bit of an appetite sharpens this process. (Shopping in a famished state, however, may result in overbuying and waste. You should experiment to see what your ideal state of readiness is.)

2. To surprise myself I try to buy something different each time, whether it's a new kind of apple or a strange root vegetable.

3. I go to the market or the store in the morning whenever possible. Not only is the selection larger but the food is fresher, not having spent the day in the sun or on the shelves. The farmer or produce person is fresher too and usually more open to conversation. I treat the ingredients attentively, never packing anything on top of fragile lettuce leaves, greens, or tomatoes.

4. I make shopping a social event whenever possible. I have noticed that nothing brings the Union Square Greenmarket alive more than a tour of schoolchildren who are often filled with enthusiasm and curiosity, which they readily communicate to the farmers. I try to do the same when I can.

5. Of course, when you are at the supermarket and the producer of the food is nowhere to be seen, mindful

selection of ingredients cannot be such an intuitive process. Generally speaking, foods that are the least processed and, if processed, produced with the fewest additives put themselves in a position to be judged on their own inherent merits. This "honest" approach always deserves your attention over more manufactured foods, which in any case, by definition, are less nutritious.

A MINDFUL STEP

This exercise is simple. Go to a farmer's market or a roadside stand (or specialty produce store) that sells the farmer's own produce and spend a leisurely half hour or more enjoying the experience. Talk to the farmer(s); ask questions. Perhaps he or she will share with you a favorite recipe or preparation method or explain the ways to tell when a particular fruit or vegetable is at its peak of freshness. Buy whatever appeals to you. The temptation when confronted with all this fresh food is to overbuy; be reasonable. Take it home and cook it that night. Salute the farmer who labored to make it possible.

A DAY IN THE COUNTRY

In September of 1997 I spent a weekend near Lancaster, Pennsylvania, on the tomato-and-pepper farm of Tim Stark. Tim is an artist-grower whose canvas is the small organic farm he tends in the rolling hills two hours west of New York City. He cultivates hundreds of varieties of tomatoes and peppers (as well as vegetables for his own use) in a landscape reminiscent of a Matisse painting, with its vibrant swatches of color provided by the myriad of heirloom (prehybrid varieties preserved by seed-saving groups and individuals) vegetables. Like most family farmers, Tim is always short of workers, especially at harvest time. In true Tom Sawyer style we (my friends Roger and Linda accompanied me) volunteered/were recruited to help with the Saturday pick at his Eckerton Hills Farms. We spent a glorious day surrounded by yellow, red, white, orange, purple, and green tomatoes in a startling array of sizes and shapes, filling wooden baskets at a beginner's pace. Just before sunset we met under a large shade tree, where the harvest was being loaded onto a pickup truck. Roger and Linda and Toby Arons, who makes salsas and hot sauces for the farm, "shopped" with me for dinner ingredients among the myriad of baskets. Without a menu in mind, we made selections based on what appealed to the senses. The harvest was spectacular. It wasn't easy narrowing our choices.

Back at the farm kitchen Roger, Toby, and I improvised a menu, then in true kamikaze style, went about executing it with almost no coordination, competing for burners, knives, and cookware, bumping into each other frequently in a smallish kitchen designed for one cook. Miraculously, the finished meal showed none of the signs of its chaotic birth. We ate the meal outside on a long table under a sky filled with stars. Every compliment about the food was deferred to Tim, who had made the meal possible with his delicious passion for growing vital food.

TOMATO TART • *Yields one 9-inch pie*

Crust

10 ounces white pastry flour

6 ounces (1½ sticks) salted butter, cold

Pinch of salt

1½ tablespoons cold water

1 egg

Filling

2 tablespoons prepared Dijon mustard

4 ounces Swiss cheese, cut into thin slices

½ pound fresh tomatoes, cut into thin slices

Salt and pepper to taste

¼ teaspoon dried thyme

To make the crust: In a food processor using the pastry blade, mix the flour, butter, and salt for 30 seconds. Add the water and the egg. Process until the dough forms a ball, about 30 seconds. Flatten the ball to a 6-inch circle. Refrigerate for 2 hours.

Preheat the oven to 375 degrees. On a smooth floured surface, roll out a thin layer of dough (less than ⅛ of an inch thick) so that it easily covers a 9-inch pie pan. Gently lift the crust and place it in the pie pan. Trim off the dough that extends more than ¼ inch over the edge of the pan.

To make the filling: Brush the mustard on the crust. Place a thin layer of cheese evenly over the whole surface. Overlap the tomatoes in a layer on top of the mustard. Sprinkle with salt, pepper, and thyme. Cook for 35 minutes. Serve hot.

Besides the tomato tart, here is what we prepared:

- Rainbow chard (with yellow, orange, and red stalks). We quickly sautéed the chard in olive oil with garlic and a squeeze of lemon juice.
- Peppers, tomatoes, and sausage with basil. A mound of multicolored sweet pepper slices, onion, and garlic were sautéed in olive oil. We added yellow and red paste tomatoes, basil, and sausage. The dish was done in ten minutes.
- Heirloom tomato salad. We took the plumpest purple, red, brown, yellow, orange, and white tomatoes and cut them into thin slices. The tomatoes were sprinkled with salt, pepper, olive oil, and vinegar and brought to the table.
- Pasta tossed with cranberry beans, garlic, and fresh thyme. Cranberry beans are a shelling variety. They make a delicious pasta sauce prepared as we did that day tossed in an olive oil–moistened pan with garlic, fresh thyme, and stock or white wine.

- Grilled steak and peppers. To complete this abundant harvest meal, we grilled steaks and sweet and spicy peppers.

ON THE HORIZON

Try your hand at tasting food without eating it. Go back to the farmer's market, the roadside stand, or a well-stocked produce section in a local store. Select a few appealing raw ingredients as in "A Mindful Step" earlier in this chapter. Bring the fresh food into the kitchen. Visualize how the ingredients will look as they cook together in the pan, sense how the flavors will combine to create a new whole, give yourself up to the alchemical process of heat that transforms the taste and texture of the food. Taste the finished dish. Repeat the process you have undertaken in your mind by cooking the food.

CHAPTER FIVE

SEEING IS
CONCEIVING

*I was looking at the fruit in the basket and I
started to feel the fruit kind of giving itself up
to the world. . . . I could feel the essence of
the fruit. I swear to you, I could. And I had to
stop myself from crying from looking at the
fruit. . . . I was so grateful for the little pome-
granates and their seeds.*

—OPRAH WINFREY,
DURING A SHOW ON RESOLUTIONS

Socrates taught that wisdom is not so much learning as re-
membering. Rather than acquiring new information, real
knowledge is a matter of breaking down or transcending the
mental obstacles that separate our conscious minds from
what we already know at some deeper level.

I think Socrates was on to something. Specifically, I believe
there are two categories of internal barriers that may prevent
you from cooking as well as you can. A mundane example
may help to clarify this. Suppose you've been told about a

great radio program that features beautiful Baroque music. It seems like receiving the program should be easy, but actually a couple of things can go wrong. For example, static can interfere with your reception, so that all you hear is noise. On the other hand, the reception may be crystal clear, but if you're on the wrong channel you might hear polka music instead of Vivaldi.

In short, the problem may be lack of clarity, or too much clarity about the wrong things. Similarly, your cooking may be impeded by insufficient concentration. Or you may be concentrating too hard on preconceived notions of what cooking should entail. Possibly you think you've got to have the most expensive utensils, or that you must use certain cookbooks and ingredients. Fortunately, there's a simple solution to both these problems.

Very simple. In fact, just one word.

Silence.

Silence is the key to meditative cooking, as it is to many forms of meditation. But silence can be misunderstood. For example, silence certainly doesn't mean you can't listen to music or talk while you cook. It's really an internal quality, an ability to get beyond the kinds of distractions mentioned above.

If you're like most people, you might think that internal silence and preparing a meal are two very contradictory ideas. Cooking may mean racing back and forth between the stove and the refrigerator, watching the clock, cleaning up spills, and hoping that everything will turn out all right in the end. When this is the case, preparing a meal is above all a goal-oriented activity, culminating in a final judgment of success or failure. But meditative cooking is more about the process than the result. It's about the experience of creation rather than an evaluation of the finished product.

You may think of meditation as a cloistered activity, requiring solitude, focused attention, and the ability to sit comfortably in a lotus position. But it's really a much more broadly defined concept. Even if you've never formally decided to sit down and officially meditate, you've almost certainly had a number of meditative experiences. Whenever time seems to stand still, whenever physical exertion seems energizing rather than tiring, whenever the journey is its own reward quite apart from the destination, a form of meditation is taking place. One purpose of this book is to show you how the activity of cooking, which many people find stressful, can take you into this unique state of mind, which is somehow relaxing and stimulating at the same time.

There are times when working in the kitchen is unavoidably a hassle, but often this is because the cook has become focused on a mindset that fosters stress. Instead of simply being yourself, you try to live up to an image of what you imagine a cook should be. Cooking then becomes a limiting rather than a liberating experience.

Around the world, various spiritual traditions have developed techniques to facilitate this unique internal silence. Many of these methods are based on a simple but very important fact: The mind can only accommodate one thought at a time. This is the foundation, for example, of all forms of mantra meditation. By repeating a single word or phrase over and over again, the meditator displaces all other thoughts from his or her consciousness. And since the mantra itself is often a meaningless syllable devoid of all associations, a form of meditative silence can be achieved.

Mantra meditation is based on sound, and other techniques use sight or touch for the same purpose. Still, their approaches emphasize awareness of breathing or the heartbeat. In India, abstract visual patterns called yantras are used to focus meditation, and massage can serve the same purpose.

There are also guided meditations in which a story or word picture helps the meditator reach a mental state that is both concentrated and relaxed. In many indigenous cultures around the world, there are deeply rooted traditions of guided meditation, in which a shaman leads a group of supplicants through a sequence of mental pictures in order to create a desired state of mind. Often this ceremony takes place before a significant undertaking by the group, such as a hunting or fishing expedition. Or the meditation may be used to heal a physical or emotional problem afflicting a specific individual. In any case, all guided meditations are designed to focus the attention of the participants in a way that enhances both their spiritual power and their practical capabilities.

The three guided meditations offered below are focused on everyday kitchen objects that might seem hardly worthy of contemplation: a loaf of bread, a glass of water, and an egg. The simplicity of the subjects of these meditations is precisely the point. By following these exercises, you will move closer to the ingredients that are the basis for everything we do, that allow us to live.

A MINDFUL LOOK

1. We have all had the experience of tasting something special, something unique that has lingered in our memories until this day. A crisp apple eaten on a fall afternoon, a slice of birthday cake and ice cream in the glow of celebration, a fish fillet from a fresh catch, a cold drink after a long mountain hike. Within that recollection, focus on your sensual experience. Write a paragraph focusing on what you tasted, smelled, felt, saw, heard, and experienced. What state of mind does this put you in now?

2. Write a paragraph describing in similar terms one or two of the ingredients of your most recent meal. In what ways are the two recollections different? To what do you attribute this discrepancy?

A MINDFUL STEP

1. THE WHOLE WORLD IN A GLASS OF WATER

Water is flowing. Every drop is made of the same substance. Water never flows divided because it knows it will flow back together in time. It is eternal. Water is powerful. Although it can be soothing, comforting and cleansing, it can also be enormous, mighty and overpowering. Its nature is constant. It is true to itself at any extreme. Water is nourishing. Without water no plant and no living creature could survive. Water is still, it can be completely still and in its stillness mirror heaven perfectly. Water is pure. It is transparent, clear needing no adornment, nor augmentation. For all these features—to be flowing, powerful, profound, balanced, nourishing, still and pure—one who would follow Tao need only emulate water in every way.

—DENG MING-DAO, EVERYDAY TAO

Flowing water is the central poetic image of Taoist philosophy. It has no form, yet it can adapt to any shape. It has no color, yet it can reflect all the colors of the rainbow. The metaphor of flowing water connotes constant change, supreme adaptability, and the paradox of nonresistance as ultimate power. For the Taoist, water is quite simply the essence of life itself.

This view of water, of course, is scientifically correct as well as spiritually powerful. Water is literally what human beings are made of, and water is certainly the most important of all cooking ingredients. Yet, as is so often the case with the most important things, we take water for granted.

Even a simple glass of water expresses the shared human experience that is the foundation principle of all cooking. To perform the meditation, set aside five or ten minutes when you can be alone in your kitchen or dining room. Nothing is required except a single glass of water. If convenient, it's best to use a colorless, transparent water glass rather than a plastic or porcelain glass or cup. Tap water should also be avoided if possible.

Begin by placing a glass of water on the table in front of you. As you look at the glass and the water within, you literally see right through it. In a sense you see nothing in the glass. Though you're aware of the water, it's only partly visible—and certainly inconsequential.

Now take a tiny drop from the glass onto your finger. If you look carefully into the drop and the lighting is right, you can see a reflection of yourself and everything in the room around you. The speck of water is like a hologram, in which the whole is present in every part. Indeed, this is more than just a visual effect. Within the glass of water before you, there are molecules and atoms from every ocean, lake, and river anywhere in the world. The water in your glass may have come from a plastic bottle on your kitchen countertop, but in a larger sense it has come to you from gentle mountain streams, churning rivers, and desert oases, from Siberian ice floes and tropical rain forests, from frothing geysers and thunderclouds filled with hail. As you place both your hands around the glass of water, try to imagine how far its contents have come, and how eventually they will disperse up into the clouds once more. How many rivers can you name? How many lakes? As you list them in your mind, be aware of the fact that something of every one of them is in that glass in front of you.

If you do this with full awareness, you'll begin to see your glass of water from a new perspective. It will become as a sacramental chalice as well as a commonplace kitchen object. It is still just another glass of water, but it's also a source of connection with the larger world.

When you drink the glass of water to complete the meditation, bring your full attention to the act. In a sense if you can taste what is in a glass of water you can taste anything. Nothing could be more mundane, more neutral, more absent of flavor, more without apparent culinary significance than drinking a glass of water, yet nothing better expresses the shared life experience that cooking really is. Though we perceive ourselves as separate, and though we inure ourselves to the unique significance of each human being, sharing food however tasteless or full of flavor brings us together, just as the rivers and streams were brought together in that now-empty glass.

2. A LOAF OF BREAD

> The surface of bread is a marvelous thing primarily because of the almost panoramic impressions it makes, as if one held in one's hand the mountains of the Alps, the Taurus or the Andes.
>
> —FRANCIS PONGE, *LE PARTI PRIS DE CHOSES*

Bread is one of those foods that contain life, that *is* life. In the book of Genesis there are frequent references to leavened bread as embodying the material support of existence. The word *Bethlehem* means "house of bread" in Aramaic. Christians are reminded of the symbolic meaning of bread every time they take Communion. "Few actors on the stage of history can have played a more significant role than bread" (Jerome Assire). Marie Antoinette lost her head when she responded to the Parisian workers' demands for bread with "Let them eat cake."

Outside of a few moments of worship in church the practical role of bread in our lives is in a state of rapid decline. In 1800 the average Berlin family spent 44 percent of its income on bread. Buying bread was like paying a big mortgage. Today in our affluent, protein-centered diets bread has lost both its central role as physical sustenance and its accompanying symbolic significance. In northern Europe bread consumption is down to one quarter of its level at the turn of the century.

In the last twenty years there has been a revival of interest in bread and baking. Every major metropolitan center has an Old World–style baker producing high-quality loaves. When you perform this meditation use a freshly baked baguette from one of these quality bakeries.

As with any food truly appreciated, in enjoying bread we can use all of our senses.

SIGHT. Hold up the loaf of bread. Look closely at the shape and the color. The crust can be smooth, rough, or sharp edged like Ponge's mountain ranges. Its colors are those of the earth ranging from gold to amber yellow to deep brown. Think of the hands that molded the loaf, that formed the shape. Pretend you are looking down from an airplane on the loaf. What do you see?

SOUND. Tap the bread. Listen to the deep sound. It communicates substantiality. With a finger push the crust. It crackles like the fire that gave the heat that baked the bread. Break off a piece of the baguette with your hands. The sharp crunch is like the sound of an axe splitting a log. Think of the yeasted dough rising to give the bread its final form.

SMELL. Smell the bread. A well-made baguette will have

many fragrances: ripe grain, cut hay, roasted almonds, sweet cream. What do you smell?

TOUCH. Bread has an unusual range of textures that are a tactile pleasure. Between the crunchy firm crust and the soft crumb is a world to be experienced. Close your eyes. What are you reminded of?

TASTE. A properly prepared baguette has four of the six tastes, as discussed in Chapter 7. Balance is the key. Each flavor should be present yet create a harmonious whole.

- Salt: Bread is made with salt and you should be subtly aware of it.
- Sweet: The starch itself has a sweet taste without any sweeteners being added.
- Bitter: The caramelized crust has a slightly bitter taste.
- Sour: The yeast imparts a sour taste to the bread.

Like wine, bread can have many different tastes. What is in your loaf?

3. THE RELUCTANT EGG

Eggs, it seems, are made to be broken, and not always intentionally. If you've spent any time in the kitchen you've undoubtedly had the experience of washing inadvertently broken eggs off the floor, the countertop, or the interior of a refrigerator. Yet the obvious fragility of the egg is deceptive. In all the world, there is really no stronger or more stable shape than the perfect oval of an egg, provided that equal pressure is applied over the entire surface. Thus, diverse feats of human engineering, from subway tunnels to airplane fuselages, have duplicated the egg's contours. The egg's remarkable combination of strength and vulnerability is a beautiful example of the complexity of nature. The object most essential for continuation of life is also among the most difficult to access.

Although they would never call it a meditation, many generations of children have performed the following exercise, often to the consternation of their parents. It's best not to try this while standing on an expensive carpet!

Hold an egg in you hand. Look at it closely. What thoughts pass through your mind? Almost certainly, you think of how easily the egg could be broken. *Egg* and *break*—the two thoughts, noun and verb, naturally follow one another.

But how easy is it to break an egg? If certain rules are followed, an egg is a very hard thing to crack. To demonstrate this, place the egg in the palm of one hand and cup the other around it. Now squeeze as hard as you can, being careful to apply equal pressure on all sides of the egg. As long as the pressure is uniform, you can squeeze as hard as you like. The egg will remain intact.

If the egg breaks, there are several possible explanations. There may have already been a hairline crack in the surface. But it's much more likely that your expectations of easy breakage proved more compelling than your intention to apply equal pressure to the shell. In the same way, negative expectations in all areas of cooking can turn a meal into a mess, even when the ingredients are perfect.

A Mindful Cook enters the kitchen with clear awareness of

this truth: There are countless variables in cooking, and most of them are within ourselves.

ON THE HORIZON: THE PERFECT TOMATO

The tomato is a masterpiece of nature. With its complex and lively flavor, rich aroma, edible skin, juicy meat, and radiant color, this beautiful plant seems to provide all that the garden has to offer. If the tomato did not exist, no other plant could really provide its singular combination of a taste that is both sweet and pleasantly acidic, and a texture that is quite mysteriously both liquid and solid at the same time.

The world contains more than two thousand varieties of tomatoes, yet most of us are familiar with only a few. The standard supermarket tomato has been biologically engineered for durability. It's designed to withstand transportation by truck along interstate highways. Unfortunately, as strength increased, flavor declined. The standard commercial tomato is now a tough-skinned, pink-to-red product whose taste seems very manufactured compared to garden-grown vegetables. But as interest in quality food has increased in recent years, health-food stores, farmer's markets, and even some supermarkets now offer a variety of tomatoes during the peak seasons of summer and early fall—and, of course, many of the best tomatoes are grown in home vegetable gardens. There are tastes ranging from intensely sweet to tangy, almost like cucumber.

For the guided meditation that follows, it's best to use a vine-ripened tomato grown in your own yard or a friend's, or purchased directly from the grower at a roadside stand or green market. The meditation should take from ten to fifteen minutes.

To begin, wash your tomato in very cold water.

Look closely at it. Then close your eyes and create a mental picture of the tomato transforming itself from a seed to a full-grown vegetable. Imagine the tomato when it was green and tiny, ripening, fully ripe, and ready to be picked.

Once you have a clear image of the mature fruit, open your eyes. Imagine that you've landed on an exotic island and that you are seeing a strange tropical fruit for the first time (remember your surprise when you first came upon a kiwi or a passion fruit). What does this strange object really look like? What are your associations to other foods? What does this exotic food taste like?

Now take a bite. Compare your anticipation with the reality. Which do you prefer? Why?

A "POACHED" EGG ON TOAST

You have had a fresh look at three very familiar foods: water, bread, and the egg. This dish combines the three focused upon ingredients in a simple recipe that is no longer quite so simple if only because we see a many-sidedness in each thing.

Boiling eggs for about six minutes produces a firm

white and a soft yolk, not unlike a poached egg. It is important to concentrate on each of the simple steps. Despite our best intentions, we can all remember countless failures with eggs, especially with the fragile yolks. Hardboiled eggs are sometimes undercooked, or the shell sticks to the white as we try to peel it. Yolks frequently break as we place them in the pan to fry them, or get overcooked if we are distracted for only a moment. There is nothing easier to cook than an egg, and almost nothing less forgiving of our inattention.

. . . .

Bring water to a boil in a saucepan. Lower the eggs carefully into the pan with a wooden spoon or ladle. Raise the heat if necessary to maintain a moderate boil. Cook according to this table.

Medium eggs	5 minutes
Large eggs	6 minutes
Extra-large eggs	6½ minutes
Jumbo eggs	7 minutes

When the time is up, pour out the water. Run very cold water into the pan for 1 minute. Tap the shell gently with a spoon or on a hard surface. Peel under cold water. In the last few minutes of cooking toast slices of the bread. Place an egg, cut in quarters, on each slice. Season with salt.

Does this simple dish do justice to everything you have experienced? Is it a letdown? Are you surprised by the sensations of the finished product? What will you carry forward to your next eggs-on-toast meal?

CHAPTER SIX

PLAYING
WITH FOOD

*In the very nature of things the relationship
between feast and play is very close. Both
proclaim a standstill to ordinary life. In both
mirth and joy dominate, though not necessar-
ily for the feast too can be serious; both are
limited as to time and place; both combine
strict rules with genuine freedom. In short
feast and play have their main characteristics
in common. . . . In play as we conceive it the
distinction between belief and make-believe
breaks down. The concept of play merges
quite naturally with that of holiness. Any pre-
lude of Bach, any line of tragedy proves it.*

—JOHAN HUIZINGA, *HOMO LUDENS*

In this chapter you'll actually begin to cook. You'll prepare a
dish that may initially be unfamiliar to you, but it's one that
combines the elements of spontaneity and flexibility that are
the essence of meditative cooking. Before we cook, however,

it's important to consider the emotional context in which cooking takes place.

The kitchen is the center of nurturing, not just of nutrition. This was even more apparent before the advent of modern conveniences, when the preparation of food was a time-consuming artisanal process, a work of handicraft. In medieval Europe, the children of the aristocracy were always raised by the kitchen staff. Years might pass without any real contact between parent and offspring. This may seem heartless to us today, but where are children happier than in the kitchen? Nowhere else provides such an enticing combination of security and mystery. For a child, the kitchen is the ultimate playroom, and play should always be a part of cooking.

Play can take an infinite number of forms, but certain elements are always present.

1. Play is free in spirit and intent.
2. Play unfolds in a restricted space. All play moves and has its being within a playground marked off beforehand either materially or ideally, deliberately or as a matter of course.
3. Play creates order, *is* order.
4. An element of tension is an important part of play. Tension means uncertainty and chance.
5. All play has its rules.
6. For an activity to be playful, the imagination must be engaged: Something must be going on at a level beyond simple physical activity.

Play focuses on the way things are done rather than how things turn out. Failure, therefore, is impossible in play (of course, institutionalized games with strict rules, which can be considered play in the broadest sense, have a strong win/lose component and failure is therefore a possibility). If there's a feeling of having failed at play, a feeling that mistakes have been made, the real mistake is that play has for some reason been allowed to turn into work. Your task is to transform your kitchen into a playroom in the best sense of the word—a place that's safe and exciting at the same time.

The process begins before you actually enter the room. Pause for a moment, and consciously put aside notions of the kitchen as a center of chaos, confusion, and messy accidents. Instead, think of it as a place where, quite literally, nothing can go wrong. This positive emotional outlook will come more easily if your kitchen has been properly prepared as a physical space. You should feel comfortable in your kitchen and not encumbered by obvious distractions.

Just as children surround themselves with the things that both excite and comfort them you can create a kitchen environment that is filled with positive reinforcement.

A few suggestions:

- A traditional European country restaurant has its entry decorated with still lifes of food of the season as well as of flowers to convey a sense of abundance and a respect for nature. The result is reassuring and welcoming to the guest. It can have the same effect on the cook. A fire in a nearby fireplace or lit candles can serve the same function.

- Arranging the raw ingredients to be prepared artfully like a tableau the way a child arranges a doll and its clothes or toy soldiers before a play battle can give a sense of possibility.

- Treat yourself as you would a welcomed guest. Put on your favorite music, pour yourself a glass of wine, adjust the lighting to be bright but not glaring. Make sure a fresh breeze lightens the room.

- Address any other concerns such as phone calls that need to be made, errands that require your attention, and so on, before you begin to cook so that the most obvious distractions are eliminated.

- Is there someone you would like to share this experience with—a playmate? By all means invite him or her into the kitchen if you think the experience will be enjoyable for both of you.

- Before you begin to cook, always be sure your kitchen is clean. This helps make every cooking experience a fresh one, and lets you see your ingredients sharply and cleanly, with no clutter to distract you from them.

- Always wash your hands before getting started.

- Take a quick inventory of the utensils and ingredients that are available. Do you have everything that you'll need?

- Are your knives sharpened? Will you have enough counter space to work cleanly and efficiently?

A MINDFUL STEP: BRUSCHETTA

This is not a recipe at all in the conventional sense, but rather a culinary celebration of a joyous time of year.

In many parts of Italy, a high point of country life is the pressing of olive oil from fruit picked in late fall and early winter. Olive oil, of course, is the most basic ingredient in Italian cooking, and a wonderful ritual has evolved to celebrate the first pressing. Oil taken directly from the spigot of the press is poured over freshly toasted peasant bread that has been rubbed with raw garlic. This bruschetta, as it is known, actually combines several essential ingredients of Italian cooking, which can be added progressively and in any order. Thus, each ingredient can be appreciated both alone and in combination with the other elements. The success of the dish depends solely on the quality of the ingredients themselves. These include:

> *Tomatoes (vine-ripened if possible),*
>   *coarsely chopped*
> *Extra virgin olive oil*
> *Fresh garlic, peeled and chopped*
> *Freshly baked bread such as a baguette*
> *Salt*
> *Pepper*

Arrange all the ingredients on individual plates in a way that is pleasing to the eye. Pour the olive oil into a clear bowl. Remove the bread from its wrapper. Take a second to look at the ingredients before you begin.

Between each tasting you may want to drink a few sips of water to clear your palate.

Slice the bread into 10 or more pieces about ½ inch thick.

The basic recipe includes tomato, garlic, and salt and pepper on toasted bread that has been dipped in olive oil. That is only a starting point, the origin of the dish. You owe no allegiance to those who invented this food except to enjoy yourself as they do when they prepare it. Let your sense of discovery take you where it will.

- To follow the herb path defined by garlic, you can add fresh basil, thyme, oregano, parsley, chervil, mint, or cilantro.

- To emphasize the sweetness of the tomato you could add a few pieces of raisin or even a little sweet fruit such as peach, nectarine, plum, or pear.

- To accentuate the acidic aspect of the tomato, spoon over a dab of balsamic vinegar or lemon juice.

- Do the same with anchovy and red pepper flakes.

Once you have established the parameters of your basic recipe, create any and all combination of these ingredients you want. The wildest ones may turn out to be the most delicious or they may not. You will never know until you try— which, after all, is one of the foundations of play, to approach the unexpected with openness.

CHAPTER SEVEN

THE SIX
FLAVORS

*The five colors blind one's eyes. The five
tones deafen one's ears. The five tastes
ruin one's palate.*

—LAO TZU, *TAO TE CHING*

When we consider the world's major spiritual traditions and
their teachings about food, two distinct principles begin to
emerge. The first of these is based on exclusion—the idea that
certain substances should be prohibited from the diet, as an
expression of piety and adherence to religious precepts. Both
Islam and Judaism, for example, strictly forbid pork and other
swine derivatives. There are also complete or partial fasts associated with various holidays throughout the year.

In contrast to this theme of prohibition and exclusion,
other doctrines emphasize inclusion and the importance of a
wide-ranging diet. Traditional Indian cooking identifies six
distinct flavors, and stipulates that ideally each meal should
include them all. The source of a particular taste—whether
sweetness comes from butter or from bread, for example—is

less important in an Indian meal than the simple fact of its presence.

For the Mindful Cook, the tradition of including a broad range of tastes is extremely satisfying because it provides us with access to a concrete way of approaching the essence of eating. Nothing is more basic to the experience of food than these building blocks.

Although it differs slightly from the Indian version, a consensus list of the tastes includes sweet, sour, bitter, salty, spicy, and plain. These tastes are all associated with specific foods, although a given food can evoke more than one. Each taste has unique benefits for cooking when present in proper proportion.

The Mindful Cook uses the concept of six flavors as a foundation for building balance and variety in a meal. And because they are on the tip of the tongue, so to speak, the experience of the six tastes can provide a way for recalling specific foods without need for written descriptions or detailed recipes.

Building balance is one of the key concepts in a sister art form, the art of wine making. My own experience with the fundamentals of wine production was centered on Champagne. I had the enviable task of writing a pocket guide to Champagne drinking. I spent a week in the Champagne region of France visiting producers and tasting their products. At a dinner given by Moët & Chandon in honor of visiting wine writers, I was presented with a gift from one of the founding families of this venerated house, the Pozzo di Borgos. In order to help wine lovers discover the original components of

Champagne and other French wines, Moët had produced a tasting kit called *Le Nez du Vin* ("the nose of wine"). It consists of a series of fragrances distilled from the natural sources of various flavors found in wine, among them apricot, coffee, lemon, apple, vanilla, hazelnut, and honey. The essences are accompanied by cards that picture the source of the perfume and enunciate which wines and which regions embody these flavors. With the kit in hand one can learn to break down the components of Champagne, for example, which is made from twenty to thirty different batches of red and white grapes, each with a different flavor, by smelling a perfume and then sipping the wine. The fusion of flavors that creates the marvelous quality of the successful blend is then all the more appreciated. We will use this technique to discover the unity of the six flavors, by tasting each of them separately and then fully assembled in a whole that is larger than the sum of its parts.

Certain culinary experiences are so deeply satisfying because nothing seems left out. But a really successful meal requires more than the simple presence of all six flavors. When the flavors exist in proper proportion, both in an individual dish and in the meal as a whole, they balance one another. The various elements of a meal maintain their identities and at the same time become a harmonious creation. To put it in other terms, the flavors tell a whole story.

Many of us have strong personal attachments to one or more of the flavors that give us an entrée into the complex relationships between food and past occurrences. Proust's madeleine passage in *Swann's Way,* where a tea cake evokes an entire universe, is different only, perhaps, in the elegance of expression from what some of us have experienced. These attachments may or may not be related to the specific social/emotional connotations of the flavors that are generally thought of as the following:

A LEXICON OF FLAVORS

> *Sweet = happy, wet, rich*
>
> *Sour = unhappy, complaining, sharp*
>
> *Bitter = resentful, lingering, melancholy*
>
> *Spicy = energetic, lively, unexpected*
>
> *Salty = difficult, harsh, dry*
>
> *Plain = ordinary, usual, frequent*

In America, classic food menus tend to be somewhat unadventurous in their inclusion of the six flavors. Perhaps this can be traced to the Anglo-Saxon character of the Founding Fathers, who sought consensus and moderation, and to the Judeo-Christian tradition, which encourages harmony and tranquility. In other cultures, particularly in Asia, contradiction, paradox, and facilitation of uncertainty mark many social attitudes and habits, including cooking.

Take a typical American holiday dinner. There is a great deal of the plain—mashed potatoes, turkey, stuffing, gravy, biscuits; a touch of the sour—vinegar or lemon in the salad dressing; and a whole lot of the sweet—pie, sweet potatoes, cranberry relish, even beets. The spicy, the bitter, and the salty are almost nowhere to be tasted. Other traditional blue plate specials have the same narrow range of flavors. Hamburgers and french fries; eggs, bacon, and toast; roast meat, potatoes, and a green vegetable. Fast food is almost entirely defined by the fat (plain) and sweet flavors it contains in overwhelming amounts. It is easy to attribute this bland cooking to the limited ingredients available in northern regions. Certainly you can't cook with what you don't have. But the most piquant food in all of China is found in Szechwan, a northern province, where sweet and sour battle each other in many dishes like the changing frontiers of yin and yang.

Indian food, like the clamorous street life of its cities, is largely based on encouraging the spicy, sweet, and sour flavors to find their own order based on the demands of the moment. While Moroccan cuisine, stemming from a culture depicted largely through the oasis, contains unexpected sweet accents in spicy or bland dishes. Latin Americans with their energetic sense of the tragic appropriately combine the sour and the spicy with occasional bitter and sweet accents. Cantonese regional cooking, with its well inscribed role as the Garden of Eden of China, artfully combines the full spectrum of flavors.

The tremendous growth in ethnic cooking and eating in America in no small part is due to the quest to experience the full range of flavors and points of view these cuisines embody.

One of my favorite dishes contains all six flavors. It is a Sicilian tomato sauce that represents a genuine Mediterranean cross-cultural collaboration. The sauce includes the sweetness of raisins and the spiciness of dried red chilies from North Africa, as well the basic flavors of Sicilian peasant cuisine: the sourness of tomatoes, the saltiness of anchovies, the bitterness of arugula, and the plainness of pine nuts and wheat-based pasta.

SICILIAN TOMATO PASTA SAUCE • *Serves 4*

2 tablespoons olive oil

6 cloves garlic, peeled and chopped

2 canned anchovies, chopped

¼ cup raisins

⅛ teaspoon red pepper flakes

¼ cup pine nuts

1½ pounds fresh Italian paste tomatoes, or one 28-ounce can of whole peeled tomatoes

2 cups arugula (or rapini/broccoli rabe or radicchio), washed and coarsely chopped

¼ cup chopped fresh parsley or basil

¼ teaspoon salt

1 pound dried pasta

In a large sauté pan, heat the olive oil. Over medium heat, cook the garlic, anchovies, raisins, red pepper flakes, and pine nuts for 2 minutes. Add the tomatoes, arugula, parsley, and salt. Simmer for 20 minutes. Meanwhile, boil salted water and cook the pasta al dente. Serve the sauce over the pasta.

A MINDFUL LOOK

1. Which of the six flavors are your favorite(s)? Which do you crave?
2. Which do you least like?

3. What connotations or emotional associations do you have for each of the flavors? What foods come immediately to mind?

4. Try to recall a food from childhood that was an early experience of each flavor. Was that experience positive or negative?

5. What are your favorite combinations of flavors?

6. What dish do you prepare that has the most flavors? What menu has the most?

7. Go back to your food journal. Do you select favorite foods according to specific tastes? If so, you may want to use some of those favorites as part of the menu to flavorize.

A MINDFUL STEP

Take one of your own favorite menus and look at ways to expand its range of flavors. Look at the dishes one at a time and together. Begin simply with soup and salad or a sandwich. As you gain confidence, expand your additions. You can do something as simple as adding a sour (lemon juice) or spicy (cayenne) accent to a soup or stew, or include a bitter green such as radicchio or a few spicy leaves of arugula to a lettuce salad.

ON THE HORIZON

Cooking is known as an art form and with good reason. On any level that it is undertaken, preparing food encourages us to use our aesthetic sensibilities to achieve a pleasing result. In the 1980s a rash of cookbooks appeared accompanied by musical selections on audio cassettes, each dish paired with a specific classical composition that was designed to enhance the dining experience. This fad was short-lived, but something meaningful resided in the core concept of relating food to music. Going beyond a simple pairing of the two frameworks, these forms share essential principles of composition. For example, employing the concept of combinations of flavors and their contrast and balance, we can return to the menu in this chapter and see the same dishes as expressions of theme and variations (the corn salsa repeating and amplifying the sweet spicy theme of the chicken dish) and of contrasting "melodies": the bitter and sour flavor of the greens throwing into stark relief the sweetness of the sweet dishes. In the nineteenth-century novel *Against the Grain,* by Joris-Karl Huysmans, the hopelessly cynical protagonist serves a dinner in which every dish is black. Translating this unity of approach into a mindful context, you could create a "musical" meal in which every dish contains two or three of the same flavors, including spicy. As the meal progresses, the spicy theme (or any of the others) could become more predominant, more distinct, more apparent. In culinary counterpoint flavors can be juxtaposed to create a pleasing dissonance. Following the form of theme and variations, flavors in the later dish can be counterpoised to the appetizer, which can be viewed as the opening statement of the main theme. Techniques of variation might include ornamentation, which implies substitution of a more extended or elaborate version of the original flavors, transposition in which the flavors are kept but with less intensity.

Compositional structure provides another way to look at the relationships of flavors. Its significance is not simply in its literal application. Any positively focused configuration that takes us outside our patterned thinking introduces the possibility of a mindful moment.

MUCH DEPENDS ON FLAVOR

In her book *Much Depends on Dinner,* Margaret Visser offers the social and gastronomic history of each dish in a traditional and gastronomically uneventful American evening meal: corn, chicken, rice, salad, ice cream. This menu is typically long on sweet and plain foods. I offer a six-flavor menu using these basic dishes as starting points.

GRILLED CORN SALSA — SWEET, SPICY, SOUR • *Serves 4*

Corn is part of the American Indian trinity of food along with squash and beans. It is the basis for hundreds of foods and food additives, many of them sweet. Corn is both a starch and a vegetable, but is almost never the raw material for a condiment as it is here. This triumvirate of flavors is the holy trinity of many spicy relishes such as chutneys and Asian dipping sauces. Within the dish, cooked corn is like the main course and raw tomatoes and chilies are the accents. The intense, sweet-spicy flavor heightens a more subtle version of the same combination in the following chicken recipe.

• •

> 8 young ears of corn, husks left on
> 2 fresh poblano or other medium-hot peppers
> 4 fresh tomatoes, chopped
> 1/4 cup fresh Italian basil leaves, chopped
> 1/4 cup cilantro leaves, chopped
> Juice of 2 lemons
> Salt and pepper to taste

Grill the corn in the husks on a barbecue or under the broiler for five minutes or until nicely browned. Roast the peppers at the same time. Cut the corn off the cob. Peel the skin off the peppers. Combine the corn, peppers, and the remaining ingredients in a bowl.

MOROCCAN APRICOT-ALMOND CHICKEN — SWEET, SPICY • *Serves 4*

Americans have a familiarity with sweet-tasting meat dishes mainly through sweet and sour Cantonese ribs, Hawaiian pineapple chicken, and ketchup-based barbecue sauces. A sweet and spicy stew is another matter. The cuisine of the Maghreb—Morocco, Tunisia, Algeria, and Libya—has its origins in the nomadic lifestyle of sheep- and goat herders. When they arrived at an oasis they would grill meat on a spit over an open fire and serve it accompanied by dates harvested from the wild palms that bordered the water. This pairing became deeply embedded in the cooking and the emotional sensibility of North Africa. Today there are hundreds of combinations of meat and fruit in traditional cooking. Each one evokes the memory of the comfort and security that come from having reached the source of life in the middle of a barren landscape.

. . . .

1 cup unsulfured dried apricots

*One 3- to 4-pound chicken, cut into eight
   serving pieces*

2 tablespoons olive oil

2 onions, peeled and chopped

1 tablespoon peeled and chopped fresh ginger

1 cup water

1 stick cinnamon

Pinch of saffron soaked in ½ cup boiling water

Salt to taste

4 ounces shelled walnuts, chopped

3 tablespoons honey

½ teaspoon red pepper flakes

Soak the apricots in boiling water for 20 minutes. In a heavy casserole, sauté the chicken in the oil. Brown evenly over medium heat. Add the onions and ginger. Heat for 3 minutes. Add the water, the apricots and their soaking water, the cinnamon, the saffron and liquid, salt, walnuts, honey, and red pepper flakes. Cover and simmer for 45 minutes. Remove the chicken to a warm oven. Reduce the liquid by one half over high heat. Serve over the rice (recipe follows) with the sauce poured on the meat.

RICE WITH PEAS, SUN-DRIED TOMATOES, AND OLIVES — PLAIN, SALTY • *Serves 4*

Rice is generally not conceived of as a carrier of complementary flavors. In fact, the word *starch* connotes a filling, bland neutrality. Potatoes, pasta, cooked grains— they are on the plate to absorb other flavors and provide substance. One of the little surprises of the balanced menu is how delicious sweet, hot, and salty flavors mingle together. This rice dish is vegetarian. It gets its flavors from Mediterranean condiments. Able to stand alone, this dish when paired with the corn relish and chicken creates a complex fusion that can be looked at and tasted from multiple perspectives. The salty rice is like the long, hot journey that ends with the arrival at the oasis.

. . . .

> 1½ cups water or vegetable stock
>
> 1 cup white rice
>
> ¼ cup sun-dried tomatoes, drained (if packed in oil) and chopped
>
> ¼ cup green olives, pitted and chopped
>
> ½ cup fresh or frozen peas
>
> Salt to taste

Bring liquid to a boil. Add the rice and other ingredients. Reduce to a simmer, cover, and cook for twenty minutes.

COOKED GREENS SALAD — BITTER, SOUR

Green salad is an appetizer served cold or at room temperature, correct? Cooking bitter salad greens such as radicchio and escarole softens their astringency and creates an unusual texture out of something very familiar. The bitter, sour flavors call into contrast the sweet hot flavors of the meat and the saltiness of the rice. In a way this dish is like a little bit of hardship (isn't that how we thought of the spinach our mothers insisted we eat?), or perhaps an obstacle along the path that offers a contrast to the immediate gratification of the main course and therefore makes us even more appreciative of its rich rewards.

. . . .

3 heads of endive, coarsely chopped
1 head of radicchio, coarsely chopped
2 cups of arugula, thick stems removed
2 tablespoons olive oil
2 tablespoons lemon juice
Salt to taste

Wash and thoroughly dry the greens. Heat the olive oil in a skillet. Add the greens and sauté just until the leaves soften. Sprinkle with the lemon juice. Add the salt. Serve hot.

VANILLA ICE CREAM—PLAIN, SWEET

This menu has so many flavors the ice cream is a simple counterpoint. Substitute fresh fruit if you are looking for a light alternative.

CHAPTER EIGHT

THE PERFECT
MISTAKE

> *You must bring freedom, relaxation, knowl-*
> *edge and imagination to the thing and, above*
> *all, do not be afraid; a failure is no disgrace*
> *and may very often be more instructive than a*
> *success. . . . The sense of failure is, in any*
> *case, always sharper in the mind of the*
> *practitioner than in those of the guests—I*
> *know that I have often diminished my table*
> *companion's pleasure in a meal that would*
> *otherwise have ravished them by a helpless*
> *compulsion to critically analyze each*
> *preparation.*
>
> **—RICHARD OLNEY, *SIMPLE FRENCH FOOD***

The perfect omelet, the perfect martini, the perfect little restaurant in the South of France—these and other perfections have occasioned countless perfect magazine pieces on aspects of food and drink. But can a mistake in cooking be as perfect as anything else? Can a mistake be more interesting, and perhaps even more flavorful, than a scrupulously executed recipe? I believe so. Moreover, I'm convinced that mistakes and our responses to them can bring us closer to cooking as a meditation than almost anything else in the kitchen.

Making mistakes while cooking, embarrassing ourselves in front of our guests, burning a dish and filling the kitchen with smoke—the horror, the horror! But the only real harm of such experiences is to our sense of cooking as an adventure. Making the same dish over and over again may seem preferable to risking another total kitchen breakdown. This, of course, would be a great mistake.

The kitchen is a space in which we expect ourselves to be perfect, because that is what we believe others expect of us. In this sense, the kitchen has resisted the nonjudgmental doctrines of recent self-development literature, which have had widespread influence in other areas, such as the athletic field, the boardroom, and (perhaps!) the bedroom. Business literature is filled with stories of apparent mistakes that have been the foundation of highly successful products. The substance known as Teflon, for example, which coats many pots and pans, was discovered by accident during a "failed" experiment on refrigeration gases in the early 1950s.

Outstanding chefs surely experience trial and error in developing new recipes, but most are reticent about this. Though a few words about experimentation may slip through in an interview, we are for the most part left to contemplate full-color, brightly lit photographs of perfectly realized creations.

In a domain where mistakes are almost never acknowledged, what is a perfect mistake? A perfect mistake is one that encourages the cook to exceed his or her past accomplishments, thereby leading to a new and often unexpected result. Many of the classic dishes and foods we take for granted today were the result of responses to unsuccessful dishes or to unforeseen circumstances. Béchamel sauce, created by Louis de Béchamel in the seventeenth century, was made necessary by the French refusal to eat salt cod imported from Newfoundland by Béchamel himself. Rather than lose his fortune, he created the masking butter-and-milk-based sauce that took Paris by storm. The Scottish grocer James Keiller purchased a large quantity of Spanish oranges at the local port at an excellent price, only to find that they were too bitter to eat. His wife suggested he add large amounts of sugar, and in so doing they created the first orange marmalade. Their family business grew into a major enterprise, using the white ceramic pots we now associate with this conserve.

Perhaps the mistake that was most easily corrected was that of American chef George Crum when he was working at Moon's Lake House, a Saratoga Springs, New York, restaurant in 1852. When a patron complained that Crum's french fries were too thick, he sarcastically responded by shaving his spuds into paper-thin chips, which he then fried . . . and later named potato chips. His patrons were thrilled. Eventually he opened his own restaurant across the lake, where the likes of Jay Gould and Vanderbilt were forced to stand in line because no reservations were taken.

If a mistake opens the territory of surprise by surprising us negatively, we can surprise ourselves in a positive way by turning the mistake into an opportunity for discovery. For Zen Buddhists in the kitchen, faults are the very best ingredients. They allow us to turn errors into victories, weaknesses into strengths. According to traditional teachings the true Zen cook can make a beautiful offering out of ingredients most people would consider to be garbage, converting a disaster into a triumph.

In the Taiwanese film *Eat, Drink, Man, Woman,* Mr. Chu, the protagonist, prepares an elaborate meal in his home kitchen, a Sunday ritual to honor his daughters that includes stir-fried squid, smoked duck, clay pot chicken, pork belly and mustard greens, steamed shrimp dumplings, and steamed whole carp and ginger. Just as the family is about to eat this feast, Chu receives a phone call from his best friend and coworker. He is needed at the hotel, their place of shared employment. The chef sprints out of the house and jumps into a cab, leaving his daughters scratching their heads. He finds his best friend and immediate assistant in the cavernous hotel banquet kitchen on the brink of disaster in the midst of preparing the wedding banquet of the governor's son. The assistant has purchased fake shark's fin, which upon cooking has dissolved into a gelatinous mass. Chu improvises a dish that resembles a classic recipe, Joy Luck Phoenix Garden. When questioned as to how he plans to pull off this save, he replies, "I don't know, but I will." And he does. The guests are thrilled, and so are we in the movie audience, who find the chef's emergency rescue mission more memorable than the Sunday banquet served to his family. His daughters also find the father's leave-taking memorable; it provides them with an unexpected respite from their filial responsibility of having to express appreciation for the Sunday routine of overabundance.

IMPROPER EXECUTION

The most common cause of kitchen failure for the amateur cook and the professional chef alike results from an error in technique. A dish is burned or raw on the inside, oversalted, underspiced, or has excessive amounts of a strong-flavored ingredient. The possibilities are nearly endless.

Not long ago, I attended a dinner at a well-known food society in New York City. On this particular night a California chef prepared a Pan-Asian meal. The appetizers and the first course were excellent. The main dish, pheasant, was also handsomely presented, but as I cut into the breast meat my knife suddenly met a great deal of resistance. As I looked around the table, I saw similarly puzzled looks on the faces of the other guests as they sawed away at their defiant birds. Clearly, something had gone very wrong in the kitchen. Perhaps the birds had been cooked at too high a temperature or roasted well beyond doneness.

At the end of the main course I observed that nearly every plate was carried out of the dining room with the meat untouched. Everyone was hoping for some explanation, but none was forthcoming. This omission was really more disappointing than the poorly cooked pheasant. Everyone makes mistakes or has a bad day; it happens to the greatest masters in any field. By failing to acknowledge that something had gone wrong, the chef missed a real opportunity. Suppose, instead of serving an inedible roasted pheasant, the kitchen had turned out an improvised dish with whatever ingredients were available? The hearts of the guests would certainly have been won over by this act of heroism. As it was, the meal was essentially ruined not only by the poorly prepared main course, but by the chef's uncourageous way of dealing with it.

FAULTY INGREDIENTS:
THE STRANGE BURGUNDY

Though it's less common than an error by the chef, a dish can also be ruined by faulty ingredients or an equipment breakdown. The best plans of a cook can be wiped out by a spoiled piece of meat or fish or a spilled sauce or a broken food processor or blender. This is less likely to happen at a restaurant, especially at a great restaurant like Chez Panisse, or so one might presume. Actually this mishap was more like an act of God, as the restaurant was in no way responsible, but it provided the context to learn how something should taste by tasting its deformation.

A meal at Chez Panisse was always a sentimental occasion for those of us who happened to live in Berkeley. After making our reservations thirty days in advance, we put ourselves at the mercy of the chefs and their selections for the seasonal prix fixe dinner. As the meal began, dinner companions typically ordered an expensive burgundy, usually one suggested by the waiter.

On one memorable occasion, however, the waiter uncorked the bottle and immediately turned his head away in seeming disgust. "It's bad," he announced, and by now the four of us at the table could smell the odor emanating from the uncorked bottle. Out of curiosity each of us took a deep whiff. Wine experts sometimes call this the Goodyear aroma, and the reference to burning tires is certainly apt. But to our surprise another table requested that we allow them to examine the off bottle.

Incredibly, our burgundy became the star of the dining room! It was passed around to every table, provoking enthusiastic commentary between dinner parties and a long string of descriptive adjectives at each stop. It seems that a completely undrinkable bottle can become a perfect mistake and thereby an excellent tool for demonstrating what can go wrong with a wine and what a wonderful thing a good bottle is. The food at that meal was memorable, wonderful in every detail, as was the replacement bottle of wine, but what remained with us for years was the strange and unexpected taste of the awful burgundy, and the sense of community it created among strangers.

It's generally much better to see your mistakes, not as catastrophes plain and simple, but as learning opportunities. Trial and error. This is how computers operate, it's how children learn, and it's even how the universe works. The great physicist John Wheeler was thinking about the evolution of the universe when he said, "The whole problem for mankind is to make our mistakes as fast as possible." But his thought can apply equally well in the kitchen.

It seems there is something in human nature that demands we do things wrong before we do them right. In many areas of life this can be truly exasperating, and deeply painful, but cooking shouldn't be one of them.

A MINDFUL LOOK

Reconstruct as literally as you can a few recent kitchen failures. You may want to create a brief written portrait as you did of your kitchen self-image. If none come to mind, either you may be avoiding challenges or suppressing unpleasant experiences. You can apply the following mishap checklist to this recollected failure and to any others that take place in the future.

1. What went wrong? Why did it happen? Was this culinary mishap due to improper execution, faulty ingredients, the caprice of an outside force, or a combination of factors?
2. Did you blame yourself in a circumstance you could have done nothing to change?
3. If you were responsible for the mistake, try to analyze it thoroughly. Was it the result of unreasonable expectations for your equipment or ingredients, of being distracted, of lack of knowledge about a technique or ingredient, of inadequate planning, of impatience or impulsiveness? In other words, what can you take away from the experience that makes you more open, more flexible, more mindful?

4. Was the failure itself irreversible? Was the dish completely ruined? Could it have been presented partially completed or somehow altered? Did an inner voice intervene at that point and demand that you reject a not ideal but perfectly edible offering?

5. In the worst case, what are the repercussions of creating an inedible dish? Did it make you less adventurous in the kitchen, less willing to take risks? What was really lost?

A MINDFUL STEP

One of the most successful character-building exercises utilized by businesses and educational institutions is some version of survival camp. Individuals voluntarily set for themselves hard-to-achieve goals in an unforgiving natural setting without many of the conveniences of urban living. When they return to their routines they find that they have a new sense of perspective about what is really important and new problem-solving skills. You can create a kind of Outward Bound Kitchen in order to develop skills that will encourage you to solve problems, turning ordinary mistakes into, hopefully, perfect mistakes.

1. Prepare a menu that would normally require three or four burners, using only one.

2. Cook a meal without using any spices (not even salt, soy sauce, ketchup, etc.) or herbs. Cook a meal without using oil or butter. Invent your own kitchen deprivation.

3. Cook a dish from no more than three ingredients that you would be willing to serve to others.

4. Select a meal that you routinely count on as a convenient time saver, such as packaged spaghetti with meat sauce in a jar. Make everything from scratch, including the pasta.

ON THE HORIZON

Take a classic recipe like coq au vin or spaghetti and meatballs in tomato sauce or beef stew. Purposefully leave out two or more of the key ingredients such as the chicken and wine in the first recipe or the tomatoes and ground meat in the second recipe. Make the dish, adding, if necessary, a few additional ingredients that do not resemble too closely what has been omitted. Name the dish something fanciful. Clever names can go a long way toward obscuring the unusual origin of a dish.

SQUID IN ITS OWN INK: A LEARNING EXPERIENCE • *Serves 4*

The most arduous perfect mistake I ever made happened during recipe testing for my first cookbook, one written on the subject of squid. (Some would say my real mistake was writing a book on such a weird topic.) Besides its ungainly appearance, the objection most often voiced to eating squid is that it is chewy at best, and rubbery at worst. In the early stages of experimentation I learned that sautés and stir-fries in which the squid was cooked less than two minutes yielded a tender result.

As I tested various stews and whole stuffed recipes I gradually increased the cooking time to ten minutes, then twenty minutes. In every case the squid was tough. There are many foods that are tender if cooked a few minutes or less, but grow progressively tougher the longer they are cooked. There are others, such as certain cuts of meat or varieties of fowl, that become more tender the longer they are cooked. None that I knew of followed an alternating cycle of tender, tough, and then tender. It just didn't seem possible.

My book was at an impasse. I would have to defy a no less reputed source than *The Larousse Gastronomique*, in which the ideal cooking time was given as fifteen minutes. Yet when I tried this French gastronomic bible's recipe for stuffed squid, which was delicious in every other regard, the meat was just as hard to cut as in any of my recipes.

My reluctance to push forward was not simply a fear of the unknown but was based in part on the embarrassment that I had experienced at each of the testing dinners, attended by a number of my friends, at which several of the courses were basically marathon chewing exercises. I had two choices: either go forward in full public view or conduct my long cooking research in private. Throwing caution to the wind, I decided to go for broke by breaking the thirty-minute slow-cooking envelope at yet another public event. For reasons still unknown to me and apparently to everyone else, thirty proved to be the magic number. A white wine–based stew slow-cooked for half an hour was wonderfully tender, even more toothsome than the sautés and stir-fries. My series of perfect mistakes gave way to a series of seafood stews and stuffed dish recipes and my book was completed soon thereafter.

. . . .

3 pounds squid

10 cloves garlic, finely chopped

4 tablespoons olive oil

$1/4$ cup finely ground raw almonds

2 cups dry white wine

Ink from the squid

$1/4$ cup chopped fresh parsley

Salt and pepper to taste

In order to obtain the ink sacs, you will need to buy whole squid and clean them. Fortunately it is a relatively simple operation. Think of it as more Outward Bound training.

Cut off the tentacles just above the eye. Discard the hard beak inside.

With the tip of the knife hold down on the plastic-like shell that protrudes from the body. Pull the body in the opposite direction. The entrails will slide out. Save the oval-shaped ink sac.

Holding the knife nearly horizontal to the cutting board, slide it along the body toward the opening, pressing down to remove any remaining material.

Slice the body lengthwise into ½-inch-wide slices.

Put the ink sacs into a sieve and with the back of a wooden spoon or spatula squeeze out the ink into a bowl.

Sauté the garlic in olive oil in a heavy pot or casserole for 2 minutes. Add the ground almonds and continue cooking for 2 more minutes. Add the white wine, ink, parsley, and salt and pepper. Simmer slowly for 5 minutes. Add the squid and cook, covered, for 30 minutes.

CHAPTER NINE

SPIRITED
COOKING

*Prana is the vital force of the universe,
the cosmic force . . . and it goes into you,
into me, with food. When you cook with
love you transfer the love into the food and
it is metabolized.*

—DR. K. L. CHOPRA

Spiritual traditions around the world have developed the notion of a life force—a vital energy that is present not only in plants and animals, but that animates the universe as a whole. In India, the life force is called *prana*. In China, it is known as *chi*. The Jewish notion of the *shekinah,* the holy spirit of God, is a closely related idea. In all these traditions, the presence or absence of the life force—its waxing and waning within our physical and spiritual selves—is closely identified with the state of our physical and psychic health. If an individual is prone to colds and flu, a practitioner of traditional Indian medicine might diagnose a diminished presence of prana. Similarly, a doctor of Chinese medicine would understand emotional problems such as depression or irrational anger in terms of blocked chi. In both China and India, teas and herbs would be prescribed to deal with the problem, and specific foods would be prescribed as well.

So the traditional concept of a life force and its influence on our health is closely linked to the food we eat, how it's prepared, and even to the benevolence and vitality of the cook. The art of cooking includes bringing out the life force in the ingredients and projecting one's own spiritual qualities into the meal. Thus, a Zen treatise on the preparation of rice instructs us to "see the pot as your own head, and see the water as your life blood."

One need not be a confirmed mystic to see the basic truth in this observation. If you're preoccupied or unhappy when you enter the kitchen, it's unlikely your cooking will be either tasty or nourishing in the true sense of the word. You'll do things in a hurry, you'll omit ingredients, and your meals will be either too hot or too cold—not just in temperature, but also in the emotions that are mysteriously but unmistakably transferred to the food.

How, then, can we bring out the best in ourselves as cooks? Below are some ideas that can help point the way. As your experience grows, you'll surely add more thoughts of your own.

- We enter the kitchen with positive thoughts and loving emotions, aware that these will be expressed in our cooking. Now we can cook with our entire being, holding nothing back.

- We create in the kitchen an ambiance that is both re-laxed and attentive. Indeed, this is our approach to all aspects of cooking.

- We cook from basic ingredients, using locally pro-duced ingredients whenever possible.

- We devote the same attention to simple cooking tasks as to more complex ones, aware that we express our-selves in every detail.

- We show respect for the blessings of nature that com-prise our ingredients. We waste little or nothing, aware of the scarcities that afflict much of the world and of the abundance that has been given to us.

- We allow for errors in our cooking, and in this way we express high esteem for our guests. We resist thinking of them as querulous food critics in search of excuses to attack. Mistakes don't upset us. We com-bine the enthusiasm and excitement of a child with the wisdom and patience of a grandparent.

- In serving the meal, we demonstrate a quiet generos-ity of spirit. We minimize personal authorship in order to include everyone in the process of creation and enjoyment.

- Above all, we realize that cooking is a self-rewarding process. No dish or meal, no matter how masterly or how awful, is an end unto itself. The spiritual cook understands that cooking—like breathing—continues as long as life.

A MINDFUL COOK, A SPIRITUAL KITCHEN

Picasso Café is an unpretentious pizza restaurant on Bleecker Street in the heart of Greenwich Village. Michael Colonna, the chef and owner, makes Roman-style thin-crust pizza in an oak-burning brick oven. The spare decor of the place gives no hint of what is to come, for the pizzas are miraculous creations: a perfect blend of crisp, moist crust; creamy, almost sweet mozzarella; and rich, spicy tomato sauce.

I had been coming to Picasso for about a year, and Michael was always in the kitchen, rolling out the dough and tending the oven with his long steel paddle. But one summer night, walking past the kitchen toward the backyard garden, I noticed that a stand-in was making the pizzas.

Around the tables, gossip swirled. Nobody could explain Michael's absence. A rumor even started that the restaurant had been sold. At home that night, I hurriedly phoned my wife, who was working in California. "It's time to leave New York," I said. "I think Picasso has changed hands."

A month later, however, I was walking by and saw Michael at his customary post. When I asked if he was working for the new owners, he laughed and responded, "I took one day off after six years and everyone thought I had sold out. At least thirty people told me that the place went downhill in the one day I was gone. I guess I can't leave again."

Michael is a wonderful example of the Mindful Cook. On the single occasion that he didn't cook, the only thing that changed was the identity of the man making the pizzas.

Everything else—the fire, the dough, the cheese, the sauce—were exactly the same. And the stand-in, an experienced brick oven pizza cook from Italy, was perfectly competent technically. The pizza looked the same, it even smelled the same. But it lacked something, the thing that made it spectacular, that made it unique.

Because he was getting used to a new system, the replacement appeared slightly on edge. Maybe there were other reasons as well. What he lacked was the giving spirit, the open sensibility, the focus of Michael. Nobody who noticed the difference could say exactly what it was, but they could all taste it.

For a chef, Michael's background is somewhat unusual. For seven years he was one of the top soccer players in Italy. As he traveled around the country he found himself observing cooks in some of the country's best restaurants. When his athletic career ended he decided to come to America and open a restaurant. In soccer he had used his legs. Now he would use his hands and his heart.

Michael has a concept of his restaurant that is both dynamic and integrated. He sees everything as a "chain reaction from the cook to the waiter to the customer. If I am happy, the person who serves the food is happy, and so is the patron. They feel like guests in my home and can get up to help themselves without feeling awkward."

Michael has developed his ever-changing pizza crust recipe by taking everything into account, from the humidity of the air to the idiosyncrasies of the oven that his father built brick by brick. None of this is exactly scientific, but it is all carefully thought out. Standing in the middle of the restaurant, Michael sees himself as its heart. In soccer he played middle halfback, and here, surrounded by waitresses and kitchen assistants, his role is the same. He controls the pace, sets the mood, and takes responsibility for every dish that leaves the kitchen. But if Michael is the heart, his mother is the soul of Picasso Café. She comes in early every morning to make the dough for the focaccio, start the pizza dough, build the fire, and create that day's mozzarella cheese from scratch. The intention of two generations of Colonnas is totally focused on the food.

Michael's mindful perspective can be summed up in these phrases: "Everyone in the pizza business thinks that quantity is what nourishes. They pile the pie high with ingredients. Quantity has nothing to do with nourishment. Only quality counts." An important part of quality is the mindful spirit of the chef.

THE MINDFUL RESTAURANT KITCHEN

Michael's wonderfully focused approach to preparing and serving food may well remind you of someone you know who runs a local delicatessen, a corner café, a neighborhood take-out establishment, a falafel stand, or the three-star restaurant in your part of the world.

In my own experience certain aspects of a restaurant communicate mindful respect for the clientele, for the ingredients, and for the art of cooking. I can sense this from the moment I walk in the door. I can feel that I'm entering a place that is comfortable, relaxed, where the people who work there feel at ease. Recently my wife and I visited a moderately priced Parisian restaurant called Petrelle, on rue Petrelle, in the tenth arrondissement. The decor was an appealingly French version of shabby chic. On each table, the owner had laid out a few of his favorite books on food, wine, and gardening. Many of these were classic works from the nineteenth century. A dog slept soundly in the corner. Never had I been to a restaurant that so quickly put guests in a serene mood with simple gestures of hospitality. The food, fortunately, was as inviting as the welcome. The menu was elaborate, but one waiter served the eight tables and the owner cooked every course. When I mentioned that the taste and color of the orange scallop roe reminded me of sea urchin, he offered to make cream of sea urchin soup two nights later. We could not refuse his offer. Need I say the dish was amazing? I have sent half a dozen friends to the restaurant and they have all had equally memorable experiences.

A MINDFUL LOOK

1. Recently I made dinner for friends after a difficult day filled with unexpected setbacks. I was harried and disorganized as I cooked. More important, one of my friends who had eaten my cooking a number of times told me after the meal that the food tasted different, less satisfying, less vital, less intense. Have you cooked a meal recently when you were unable to

focus on the task at hand, for whatever reason? Do you remember your experience and the outcome?

2. In contrast, most of us can remember cooking for a sick friend or relative, perhaps nothing more than the proverbial bowl of chicken soup. The act itself has a focus based on its healing intent. Contrast that medicinal cooking event with the one in which you were distracted. Try to articulate clearly the differences in how you felt and acted.

A MINDFUL STEP

There are many ways you can help yourself to focus your intentions in the kitchen. Here are three, but as you put them into practice you're sure to think of more.

1. Devote some time to making your kitchen a more pleasant place to be in. Take an inventory of what is missing, what can be changed, what you no longer use that is taking up space. Make yourself feel comfortable.

2. Spend twice as long cooking one of your favorite menus as would be your normal habit. Take the extra time to relax while you appreciate everything involved in the preparation and presentation.

3. Select one of the old standby recipes you make from memory. Visualize yourself preparing it and, at the same time, write down the recipe in a way that would be clear to another cook. Give the recipe to a

friend and see if she or he can follow it well enough to make the dish. Eat the dish with your friend.

TIELLA DI COZZE–BAKED MUSSELS AND POTATOES • Serves 4

I love the spirit of Angela, Michael's mother, as it is manifest in the wonderful yeast doughs she makes for the restaurant. I knew she must have many wonderful recipes from the old country in her repertoire. I asked her, through Michael, to give me one of her favorite dishes. As he assembled the ingredients I told Michael that I had a sense he was preparing a variant on paella. He insisted that was impossible, since this was one of his mother's favorites, an Italian classic. We left it there—that is, until I checked Waverley Root's *The Food of Italy.*

Tiella di Cozze has its origins in the seaport of Bari, the center of the province of Puglia in the southeast of Italy, where Michael's family comes from. Tiella derives from the Spanish word *paella,* which is the name of the large, two-handled cast-iron pot used in the preparation of this dish. It is one of the few foods of Iberian origin in the Italian repertoire, combining as it does seafood and rice. As it turns out the Spanish governed the city for a brief period, ending in 1647. When they ran out of ways to raise revenue they decided to place a tax on flour. The Italians threw up their hands, said mama mia, enough, and started to fight. Two weeks later the Spanish left with their tails between their legs. What survives is this dish. To the Puglians what is important is the potatoes, not the rice, unlike the Spaniards, who insist that rice is the heart of paella.

At that moment it occurred to me that through Michael's focus I had somehow been given a glimpse of the "past life" of the dish. Of course you could say that I had no such experience, that I was just respond-ing to the ingredients themselves. When I told Michael about my findings, he smiled broadly and said, "That is amazing. Something really happened in the kitchen."

. . . .

3 yellow onions, peeled and chopped

4 cloves garlic, chopped

4 tablespoons olive oil

8 large red potatoes, peeled and cut into $^1/_4$-inch-thick slices

1 pound long-grain white rice

$^1/_2$ cup chopped fresh parsley

2 tablespoons grated pecorino or Romano cheese

6 fresh tomatoes, chopped

2 pounds mussels, cleaned

Salt and pepper to taste

1 quart boiling water

$^1/_2$ cup bread crumbs

Preheat the oven to 350 degrees. In a frying pan, sauté the onions and garlic in half the olive oil until golden brown. Line a large baking dish with half the onions and garlic. Cover with the potatoes. Add the rice and half the parsley and cheese. Add the tomatoes and top with the remaining cheese and parsley. Cover with the mussels, salt, and pepper. Carefully add the water. Top with bread crumbs and the remaining olive oil. Cover with foil. Bake for 30 minutes. Remove the foil and continue baking for 20 minutes. Turn the oven to high and brown the bread crumbs under the broiler. Remove from the oven and let the finished dish rest for a few minutes. This dish can be served hot or at room temperature.

CHAPTER TEN

THE APPRECIATED MEAL

> The Power of the Lord is manifested in his
> ability to control food: to feed is to bless, to
> confer life. . . . The Lord's word is equated
> with food. Eating joins people with the Lord or
> separates them.
>
> **—GILLIAN FEELEY-HARNIK,**
> **THE LORD'S TABLE**

Every meal should be appreciated, but, alas, some meals are more appreciated than others. Throughout much of human history—and today as well, in distressingly large areas of the world—famine and starvation were constant threats. Having anything to eat, let alone enough, was recognized as a gift from God. Today each of the world's great religions sets aside periods of fasting, which are often followed by a major feast.

Endowing every ingredient, every dish, and every meal with full appreciation is a worthy goal of the Mindful Cook, but it's a goal that's best achieved gradually. As we've discussed, the religions of the world have consecrated various feast days as a way of fostering appreciated meals, but we don't really have to wait for Easter or Passover to enjoy food with full spiritual awareness. We can always create our own holidays and our own very meaningful rituals. In fact, it's an excellent way to exercise the ingenuity and playfulness that characterize the Mindful Cook.

Each of us is blessed with events and with people worthy of acknowledgment, of commemoration. While major holidays have shared significance for all of us, part of the pleasure of creating appreciated meals is that they allow us to invest our own experience with meaning. Each appreciated meal I make, coming from my experience, will be different from each one that you make. Still, certain elements are shared.

A truly appreciated meal includes three key elements:

RESPECT Each dish, and the ingredients that comprise it, is valued and treated with care. In an appreciated meal, nothing is taken for granted.

FOCUS This is really a defining characteristic of the Mindful Cook. Being focused in the kitchen doesn't mean just being careful in the sense of trying to avoid mistakes. It means having *full awareness.* Nothing is done simply by rote. Like many artists in many mediums, the Mindful Cook has the ability to approach even routine tasks as if they were being performed for the first time.

INTENTION In the law, intention is taken into consideration when evaluating any action. If a person intends to do good, he or she is immediately placed in a different category from someone who performs the same act but intends to do harm. Similarly, the quality of a dish can't be separated from the intentions of the cook. Although this may be difficult to prove in a scientific experiment, it's an important principle of mindful cooking. If a cook prepares and serves a dish without the intention that it will be nourishing in every sense, it's doomed to be the culinary equivalent of airline food. Case closed!

The film *Babette's Feast* provides a beautiful depiction of an appreciated meal. After decades of work on behalf of the two devout spinster sisters who had taken her in as a political refugee after the fall of the Paris Commune, Babette wins a substantial sum in the lottery. She uses her entire winnings to create an appreciated meal for the sisters and their fellow ascetics. The meal commemorates Babette's distant past as a Parisian chef through the dishes that were most important to her: turtle soup, caviar and crème fraîche on blinis, game birds stuffed with foie gras and truffles in pastry, rum cake, fresh fruit. The meal expresses deep thanks to the sisters. Her efforts reaffirm her affection for her honored guests and at the same time challenges them, demonstrating the ability of the appreciated meal to unify, to heal, and even to provoke.

A DISH A DECADE

Watching *Babette's Feast* coincided with the approach of my fiftieth birthday. The two events encouraged me to create a meal of gratitude, to honor people who have inspired me in my life. Some have cooked for me, others I cooked for.

I decided to select a dish for each ten-year period of my life. Since I was born near the end of a decade, this coincided nicely with the century's divisions.

This dinner encourages me to unify an appreciation of

people who have positively influenced my social and culinary life with an acknowledgment of the specific foods that I shared with them in some way, and that I cherish. This loving unification of individuals and foods is at the heart of the gratitude the appreciated meal helps express.

1950s: CHOCOLATE MALT • *Serves 2*

Not surprisingly, for the food of my early years I have selected dessert. One of my fondest memories in the kitchen came not so much from a taste as from an appliance. My father had worked as a soda jerk as a teenager, and he would fondly recall the appearance of the first gleaming chrome malted milk machine at the malt shop. As soon as consumer models were made available, he bought one. The recipe was very simple. The real pleasure came from the fact that beginning at about age eight I could mix it myself. This was my first "cooking" experience.

· ·

Three scoops of chocolate ice cream

1 pint whole milk

1 tablespoon malted milk powder

1 banana, cut into chunks

Blend all the ingredients until thick and smooth.

I couldn't have done it without you, Dad.

1960s: PAN-FRIED SAND DABS • *Serves 4*

As a college student in the late sixties, I worked part time as a commercial fisherman on Monterey Bay. My first job was on a small lampara net boat owned by a first-generation Sicilian immigrant, Salvatore Mazzarino. Our catch was the small, round, rainbow-colored fish called pompano that inhabits the turbulent waters just off the beach. The easy part was catching the fish, from a few hundred pounds to a ton every night. Then the real work began. Floating offshore at the edge of the surging breakers at three to four in the morning by the light of the deck lamp with the diesel fumes blowing in our faces, we would sort each fish and place it in the appropriate wooden box. It sounds easy, except that we had five categories—small, medium, large, extra large, and extra jumbo—and the difference in size between the smallest and the largest fish was only a couple of inches. Every time we threw a "jumbo" into the "extra-large" box and Salvatore saw it, he would yell at us: "What, you crazy? You costin' me money." Suffice it to say there was no winning an argument with this wild Sicilian.

The fish that we took home for ourselves were the odds and ends in the net other than pompano. A sand dab is a small delicate flatfish, a classic dish of the turn-of-the-century San Francisco grill restaurants such as

Tadich's and Jack's. Its sweet flavor is preserved through a minimal approach. After a night on the ocean we would return home, clean our portion of the catch, and make a simple breakfast. You can substitute a small sole, surf perch, or a freshwater pan fish.

Salvatore, wherever you are, this is not gonna costa you nothin'.

. . . .

 1 egg, beaten
 ¼ cup milk
 2 pounds whole sand dabs, cleaned
    with heads cut off
 1 cup flour
 1 cup bread crumbs
 Butter or oil for sautéing
 Lemon wedges

In a bowl, beat the egg and milk together. Dredge each fish in flour. Then coat with the egg mixture and roll in bread crumbs. Sauté the fish in butter until lightly browned. Serve with lemon wedges.

1970s: GRILLED CHICKEN LIVERS
AND BELL PEPPERS • *Serves 4*

My wife Terrel's pregnancy with our first child provided the occasion for some serious nutritional research. It led us to conclude that the key to having a healthy baby is a diet rich in protein, folic acid, iron, and calcium. One of the best sources of both protein and iron is liver. It is often recommended that women, particularly borderline anemics like Terrel, eat liver once a week. This task is not for the faint of heart. I did my best to keep things interesting on the liver front. One of our favorites was chicken livers marinated for a few hours in olive oil, lemon juice, garlic, and cayenne, grilled over a fire or under the broiler on skewers with bell peppers and pearl onions. Nine months and thirty or so plates of liver later, our son was born. For what it's worth, he started out healthy and has remained so to this day. This course is for Terrel, who managed to eat all that liver, and for my son, Beau, who most certainly benefited from it.

. . . .

3 tablespoons olive oil

Juice of 2 lemons

3 cloves garlic, chopped

Cayenne to taste

Salt to taste

1 pound chicken livers

12 pearl onions, peeled

4 bell peppers, cut in half

Preheat the broiler or make a fire in the barbecue. In a bowl large enough to hold the livers, combine the oil, lemon juice, garlic, cayenne, and salt. Add the livers and marinate for about 20 minutes, or until the barbecue is ready. Skewer the onions and peppers together on presoaked wooden or metal skewers. Spit the livers separately. Grill or broil the peppers and onions, turning frequently. Baste with a little of the marinade. When the vegetables are nicely browned, grill or broil the livers. Cook the livers for no more than 5 minutes. They should be pink inside.

1980s: BABY LETTUCE SALAD WITH VINAIGRETTE • *Serves 4*

In the early 1980s we lived in a large, rambling house in the flats of Berkeley. We had one of the largest unbroken backyards in the area, about one half acre. Down the block a smaller yard had been turned into a lettuce garden for the fabled Chez Panisse restaurant. The farmer, Andrea, a tall, Nordic-looking woman who had been a waitress at the restaurant, would talk to me over the fence about our shared interest in food. Eventually she asked if we would rent her our backyard as well. Thrilled at the idea, we suggested grazing rights as compensation. A deal was struck. For the next two years we had baby lettuce salad (mesclun) at our beck and call.

My daughter, Scarlet, grew up eating salad and to this day it is her favorite food. For this greening of my life I am grateful to Andrea Crawford and Alice Waters.

. . . .

4 cups lettuces—red and green oak leaf, red and green romaine, salad bowl, bibb, lolla rossa

2 cups bitter greens—escarole, cresses, arugula, dandelion, radicchio, curly endive

Edible flowers—nasturtiums, lavender, and violets

1 small loaf French bread, cut into ½-inch slices

2 cloves garlic, peeled

¼ cup extra virgin olive oil

2 tablespoons balsamic, raspberry, or red wine vinegar

Salt and pepper to taste

Wash and thoroughly dry the greens and flowers. Put in a bowl in the refrigerator while you make the croutons and dressing. Toast the French bread. Rub with the whole garlic cloves. Mix together the oil, vinegar, and salt and pepper until thoroughly blended. Add the croutons to the greens. Pour the dressing over the salad to taste and gently toss.

1990s: TOMATO CHUTNEY • *Serves 4*

In the summer of 1995 a Santa Monica theater mounted a retrospective of the works of the Indian filmmaker Satyajit Ray. After the first film, with its wonderfully moving rendition of daily life in rural India, I was moved to create a series of after-theater dinners for the four subsequent showings we attended, each based on the regional cuisine of the locale of that evening's film. The theater was a few blocks from our house. One night we watched the film *The World of Apu,* set in Calcutta, and then walked over to eat a meal that included a Bengali tomato chutney based on a recipe from Madhur Jaffrey's *A Taste of India.* The unusual taste of this relish, a sweet, nutty, pungent flavor, comes from the combination of dried apricot, garlic, fresh and dried chilies, tomato, and a pungent spice mixture called panchphoran. Ray is a brilliant filmmaker. His works, along with the films of Fellini, Antonioni, and Godard, were among the most important artistic influences of my youth. I was thrilled by the opportunity to extend the experience of the evening into another dimension.

. . . .

> One 1-inch piece fresh ginger, peeled
>
> 2 tablespoons oil
>
> 1 teaspoon panchphoran spice mixture (or equal parts cumin seed, black mustard seed, fennel seed, and fenugreek seed)
>
> 2 dried red chilies, ground
>
> 6 cloves garlic, chopped
>
> 1 pound fresh tomatoes, chopped
>
> 1 teaspoon salt
>
> ¼ cup sugar
>
> ¼ cup dried apricots

Cut the ginger into slices and then mince. In a skillet, heat the oil. Add the panchphoran. When the spices pop, add the red chilies, ginger, and garlic. Stir for a few seconds. Add the tomatoes, salt, and sugar. Simmer until thick, about 20 minutes. Add the apricots. Simmer an additional 10 minutes. Serve at room temperature.

In closing I would like to relate the story of an appreciated meal that was prepared by my sister-in-law to commemorate the eightieth birthday of her father who had passed away six months before. The food served was not something I would ever prepare or even eat. It was made from processed and packaged ingredients with no culinary or nutritional significance. Yet the spirit of the meal, its intent, somehow transcends the food's mass-produced origins.

Holbrook had cared little about food. He was a man on the go, filled with energy—and filled also with whatever "junk food" happened to be handy. The commemorative meal, therefore, included Hi-Ho crackers, lime Jell-O embedded with cream cheese balls covered with chopped walnuts, Campbell's tomato soup, iceberg lettuce with bottled bright-red French dressing, and a store-bought cowboy-themed vanilla and chocolate birthday cake.

As the family sat and stared at the sheer intensity and wackiness of the brightly colored convenience food of a now distant era, they felt the strong presence of the dear departed in the room. "He wouldn't have expected us to finish eating it," my sister-in-law said. "Just the fact that we remembered him in this way would have thrilled Dad. He never paid attention to who ate what, and he wouldn't now."

I never thought I would say it, but somehow it seems appropriate: long live lime Jell-O!—and the memory of Holbrook.

A MINDFUL LOOK

For many of us, holidays or special events (weddings, anniversaries, christenings) do not simply signify the pleasures of companionship, respect for a higher logic, and food. Other less pleasant social and culinary connotations born of obligation and habit come to mind. In a way appreciated meals give the opportunity for a fresh start. You are free to serve whatever you want and invite whoever pleases you.

1. Make a list of everything you liked and did not like about holiday or special-event meals you created or attended over the last few years. Include the nature and depth of the implicit and explicit shared sentiments, the relations among the guests, the food.

2. Think of concrete ways to improve on the elements of these meals you found lacking, and to bring forward what you cherished. You can do this through who you invite and how you invite them; what you serve and how you serve it; what you say, if anything; and how you arrange the table.

A MINDFUL STEP

Return to the food history you recorded in Chapter 2. Focusing on the narrative aspect, come up with a menu that is meaningful to you, that brings to life and gives another dimension to important events. This menu should not only be satisfying because It features food you love to eat, it should also help you evoke life experiences that have special significance and are therefore worth memorializing. Prepare the meal for people who will appreciate your purpose. As you serve the dishes, briefly explain their significance.

ON THE HORIZON

Create and execute a menu for friends in which the event commemorated is not identified at the outset. Perhaps you might choose a moment in your life that seemed problematic at the time, such as a setback or mishap that led to a new period of growth. At some point near the end of the meal you can explain the significance of the dishes to your guests. (Salty food is an obvious way to portray tears, bitter food disappointment, sweet and sour conveys the bittersweet, etc.)

CHAPTER ELEVEN

RIFFING IN
THE KITCHEN

*Improvisation is at war with the printed word.
It either defies analysis or, in accepting it,
finds its wings clipped.*

—RICHARD OLNEY, *SIMPLE FRENCH FOOD*

*How does one learn improvisation? The only
answer is to ask another question: what is
stopping us? Spontaneous creation comes
from our deepest beings and is immaculately
and originally ourselves. What we have to express is already with us, is us, so the work of
creativity is not a matter of making the material come, but of unblocking the obstacles to
its natural flow.*

—STEPHEN NACHMANOVITCH, *FREE PLAY*

No matter what the setting, no matter what meal has been cooked and served to them, my guests always return to the notion that the thing they admire most about an accomplished cook is his or her ability to go into a kitchen without a prearranged plan and perform "magic" by transforming a few odds and ends into a meal. In a way it is not an accident that this act is seen as a kind of alchemy because it seems beyond our understanding.

For the Mindful Cook improvisation is a mindful act, plain and simple. In many ways it is the summation of the narratives and exercises presented in this book. The purposeful meditational techniques intended to allow the ingredients to assert their uniqueness presented in Chapter 4, the centering exercises that preclude cooking offered in Chapter 5, and the experience of balancing the six flavors in Chapter 7 create a foundation of openness and receptivity the improvising cook can rely on. In negative terms this means that the Mindful Cook does not immediately superimpose habits, fears, or prejudices on a new set of culinary possibilities.

What, then, does the Mindful Cook do to create without a script besides being open and focused? Creativity is based on something. That something is life experience, the daily events, impressions, and thoughts that the artist experiences. It is wonderfully fortunate that in the arena of cooking we all have such a life experience to draw upon. Creating a food history, collecting a food diary and preparing an appreciative meal focuses us on our own food heritage.

Improvisation flows most easily when we strike a balance between openness to the moment and appreciation of the past. You can think of them as form and content. Neither mode can dominate. We honor our past by transforming it.

In his classic research the psychologist Carl Rogers identifies three personal traits consistently associated with creativity: (1) Openness to new experience; (2) reliance on internal criteria of evaluation; (3) a willingness to play with elements and concepts, to transmute, transpose, transform the given. In addition he cites two external prerequisites: (1) Psychological safety, a sense that risk taking and innovation will not jeopardize one's sense of worthiness in the eyes of the community; and (2) psychological freedom, a sense that no matter what one does, no recrimination will be experienced.

All of these attributes are completely consistent with a mindful approach. They focus on the practical, ego-oriented side of openness and flexibility. Their pursuit can provide another way into and past a challenging moment, as we shall see.

A MINDFUL LOOK

The purpose of this exploration is to locate and identify some of the impediments to invention you carry with you.

1. Picture yourself in a white-walled room with high ceilings, flooded with overhead light. Wooden work tables are filled with creative materials: oil and acrylic paints, crayons, pastels, drawing pencils, collage elements, brushes, paper, canvas. Make this visualization as complete as possible in both physical

and mental detail. From these materials (or any others you can imagine) you can make anything you want. There are no rules, no goals, no expectations. You will turn the finished product over to no one. At the very moment you are about to begin in your mind, take a step back. Identify the kinds of resistances that would come into play for you at that moment, for example, fear of looking foolish, of entering new territory without an agenda, of running out of time, of not doing as well as others, of not living up to your own expectations, of disappointing others, of having no ideas, of having too many ideas, of having ideas but not being able to realize them, of having frivolous ideas, and so on. Make a list of each impediment. How would it operate in the creative arena of the kitchen?

2. Chapter 8, "The Perfect Mistake," focuses on the situation in which plans go awry. In this chapter there is no initial plan to go awry, no objective standard by which to measure what you create. For some people this "flying without instruments" is intimidating. Most of us can remember particular moments when we learned to be wary of this open-ended approach. What was the single greatest "failure" you can recall in the improvisational arena in or out of the kitchen? How has that experience altered your perception of your talent for invention? Looking back, do you see how you might have transformed that situation into a positive experience?

A MINDFUL STEP

Improvisation is a creative approach we apply to many situations. If you play an instrument you have probably participated in a jam session where you ended up making music that surprised you. If you write, you may have used some variant on automatic writing in which you record whatever comes to mind and found that what you came up with had merit. If you are a traveler, you may have gotten lost and figured out how to get back by allowing yourself to try an unlikely route. As a parent you may have come up with a crazy scheme to get your child to stop crying that worked. Letting go in each case produced a positive result.

In this exercise you will put into action this approach with a familiar food. Select a dish with which you are totally familiar, one you make frequently, the more frequently the better. Your past experience with that dish will be like a musician playing scales. You already know the basics backward and forward.

Now create a variation on the dish, one that differs in some important way from the original recipe. Let go of your preconception of how this dish should taste, of what others expect of you, of what is most familiar and ingrained. It will be there anyway. Surprise yourself.

For example, you may want to make a beet dish with fish, re-create a hot soup as a cold one, make a vegetarian dish out of a meat recipe, turn scrambled eggs into an omelet. Change the form, change the ingredients, change the spicing; make it different, make it new.

ON THE HORIZON

For this exercise the outcome is, of course, much less important than what happens along the way.

Collect a group of friends who are keen on having an adventurous dinner party. Have each of them bring two or three ingredients from different categories. For example, one person might be responsible for herbs, another vegetables, a third the main ingredient, the fourth ingredients for a sauce, and so on. There should be no coordination among the parties. Now all you have to do is make dinner based on what your friends have purchased.

TUNISIAN TUNA SALAD • *Serves 2*

This dish appeals to me because it takes one of the most ubiquitous, bland foods—canned tuna—and turns it into something exotic and spicy. When I was young and a frequent visitor to the Left Bank of Paris, my favorite budget meal was a spicy, salty tuna sandwich served on a hard roll offered up by one of the little Tunisian sweet shops that filled the side streets of the Latin Quarter. Its 6-franc price (8 francs to the dollar at the time) made it a tasty and filling bargain. It has great appeal for Americans today because it is made without oil.

. . . .

1 can water-packed albacore tuna, drained

Juice of 2 lemons

*2 tablespoons Mediterranean black olives, pitted
and chopped*

1 tablespoon capers

1 tablespoon mild pickled Italian peppers, chopped

1 roasted mild red pepper, chopped

Cayenne or red pepper flakes to taste

French bread slices

Sliced purple onion

Sliced tomato

Arugula leaves

Mix the tuna, lemon juice, olives, capers, pickled and fresh peppers, and cayenne thoroughly. Serve on toasted French bread slices with purple onion, tomato, and arugula.

THE AUTHOR IMPROVISES

In some fundamental ways improvisation is not much different for me than for the beginning cook. I enter a strange kitchen having no idea what I am going to make, which is always a little daunting. I am initially stumped by the seemingly random array of ingredients, since the selections are not mine. Eventually something clicks and a few dishes suggest themselves. I eliminate some for arbitrary reasons (I had the same ingredient two nights ago, someone I am cooking for that night hates beans), others for aesthetic or personal reasons (I hate the color yellow), and finally settle on a simple menu. I go over it in my mind to make sure it makes sense as a series of dishes and then begin to cook.

My criteria for choosing a playground, a space to improvise in, are simple. Does it belong to someone who knows me well enough that he won't feel ill at ease when I start poking through his larder, and does he have enough basic ingredients to insure that I can come up with something we can all enjoy eating? My sister-in-law, Christie Fountain, seemed perfect. Christie loves to cook. She shops for ingredients meal by meal but has a well-stocked pantry she constantly replenishes. And she knows my kitchen manner.

CHRISTIE'S KITCHEN

MEAT	STARCHES	CONDIMENTS
Chicken breasts	*White and brown rice*	*Olive paste*
		Sun-dried tomatoes
PRODUCE	*Black beans*	*Olives*
Garlic	*Wild rice*	*Capers*
Shallots	*Split peas*	*Cilantro chutney*
Ginger	*Pasta*	*Pistachios*
Celery		*Raisins*
Lemon	CANNED FOODS	*Peanuts*
Lime	*White beans*	*Parmesan cheese*
Mushrooms	*Chickpeas*	*Canned green*
Parsley	*Tomatoes*	*jalapeños*
Carrots	*Vegetable stock*	*Powdered cumin*

There was almost nothing in her freezer and little in the cupboard beyond staples. A colorful selection (red, brown, orange) of Dutch hothouse sweet peppers caught my eye. Their bright intensity and warmth held my attention the way a bouquet of flowers draws the gaze in a still life. Following my inspiration, I decided to organize the meal around the peppers. I love the flavor of them roasted with their slightly burned sweetness. Running through my personal repertoire of pepper dishes (not a very long list), I selected a simple Moroccan cooked pepper salad. Now I had a theme or motif to follow—in this case North Africa. Some chicken breasts, a neutral ingredient if ever there was one, could be flavored with cumin, ginger, hot pepper, garlic, and lemon to continue the story. I added the salty olive paste to the chicken dish, really only thinking to bring the meal into balance, and surprised myself in the process. Now I had a meal with the salty, hot, and sour flavors of the chicken and the sweetness of the peppers (and a carrot salad that was a horizontal extension of the bell peppers). The bitterness of the greens completed the flavors.

This approach of: (1) being inspired by an ingredient(s), (2) selecting a thematic motif that justifies, supports, and extends that passion, and finally, (3) balancing the flavors comes as close as anything to articulating my own method of improvisation.

SPICY LEMON-OLIVE CHICKEN • Serves 4

4 chicken breasts, split in half

Olive oil

6 cloves garlic, chopped

2 inches fresh ginger, peeled and chopped

4 shallots, peeled and chopped

1 teaspoon ground cumin

1 tablespoon olive paste (tapenade)

2 tablespoons canned jalapeños, chopped or to taste

8 black olives, pitted and chopped

1 bunch parsley, chopped

Chicken or vegetable stock

Salt and pepper to taste

Juice of 2 lemons

In a large skillet, sauté the chicken breasts in olive oil until lightly browned. Add the garlic, ginger, and shallots to the pan. Sauté for 3 minutes. Add the cumin and cook over low heat for 3 minutes, stirring with a wooden spoon. Add the olive paste, jalapeños, olives, and parsley. Add 2 cups or more of the stock, the salt and pepper, and the lemon juice. Cover and simmer for 30 minutes. Remove the chicken to a warm plate. Reduce the sauce by half over high heat. Serve over rice.

ROASTED PEPPER SALAD • *Serves 4*

> *6 bell peppers*
> *2 cloves garlic, peeled and chopped*
> *Juice of 2 lemons*
> *4 tablespoons olive oil*
> *½ bunch fresh parsley, chopped*
> *Salt and pepper to taste*

Roast the peppers over the burners of a gas stove or under an electric broiler, turning frequently with tongs. When the skins are thoroughly charred, place the peppers in a plastic bag and seal tightly. After 5 minutes of steaming, remove the peppers from the bag and rub off the skin. Slice the peppers and place them in a bowl. Add the garlic, lemon juice, olive oil, parsley, salt, and pepper. Toss thoroughly.

CARROT SALAD • *Serves 4*

> *6 carrots, peeled and finely grated*
> *1 teaspoon ground cumin*
> *Juice of 2 lemons*
> *Olive oil*
> *Salt and pepper*

Toss all the ingredients together.

SAUTÉED COLLARD GREENS • *Serves 4*

6 cloves garlic, peeled and chopped

Olive oil

*1 large bunch of collard or other greens,
    stems removed*

2 tablespoons balsamic vinegar

Sauté the garlic in the olive oil for 3 minutes. Add the greens and stir. Add the balsamic vinegar. Cover and simmer over lowest heat for 30 minutes.

**ADDITIONAL RECIPES FROM
CHRISTIE'S KITCHEN**

MEXICAN CHICKEN SAUTÉ • *Serves 4*

4 chicken breasts

Olive oil

6 cloves garlic, peeled and chopped

2 inches fresh ginger, peeled and chopped

4 shallots, peeled and chopped

½ pound mushrooms, chopped

1 bunch parsley, chopped

4 carrots, peeled and chopped

2 tablespoons canned jalapeños, chopped

1 tablespoon capers

2 cups chicken or vegetable stock

Salt and pepper to taste

Follow the same steps as for the Spicy Lemon-Olive Chicken.

OLIVE-CHICKPEA PASTA SAUCE • *Serves 4*

6 cloves garlic, peeled and chopped

4 sun-dried tomatoes, chopped

Olive oil

12 Greek or Italian black olives, pitted and chopped

One 16-ounce can chickpeas, with liquid

2 tablespoons canned jalapeños, chopped

1 bunch parsley, chopped

1 cup chicken or vegetable stock

Sauté the garlic and sun-dried tomatoes in olive oil. Add the rest of the ingredients. Simmer covered for 20 minutes. Serve over pasta with Parmesan cheese on the side.

CURRIED SPLIT PEAS
WITH WILD RICE • *Serves 4*

2 cups uncooked wild rice

¼ cup shelled pistachios

½ cup raisins

2 sticks cinnamon

4 shallots, peeled and chopped

2 inches fresh ginger, peeled and chopped

6 cloves garlic, peeled and chopped

Olive oil

4 cups vegetable stock

1 cup split peas

2 teaspoons ground cumin

1 bunch fresh parsley, chopped

2 tablespoons canned jalapeños

Salt and pepper to taste

Cover the rice with 6 cups water. Add the pistachios, raisins, and cinnamon. Simmer covered for 45 to 50 minutes.

Sauté the shallots, ginger, and garlic in olive oil for 5 minutes. Add the stock and then the rest of the ingredients.

Simmer covered for about 45 minutes. The split peas should form a thick paste. Serve over the wild rice accompanied by cilantro chutney or tomato salsa.

A FINAL RIFF

More than anything I hope that the pleasures of improvisation, like play, are self-evident. In a way the recipes presented here are superfluous since a central theme of this chapter is that the joy of improvising in many ways surpasses the satisfaction that comes from following the formulae of other cooks. It would be in keeping with the spirit of the Mindful Cook if we were to print the recipes in disappearing ink so that after three months you could replace them with your own.

CHAPTER TWELVE

TEA, WEST
AND EAST

*How great it would be when asked,
"Where do you live?" to be able to reply,
"All over the world."*

—SOSHITSU SEN, *TEA LIFE, TEA MIND*

*Each occasion is special. Every time you plan
a tea happening, certain dynamics come into
play. Listen and hear the message. For long
after the event there is a lingering intimacy.
Three sips into a sincere tea ritual could
change our attitudes about the way we
choose to live our lives.*

ALEXANDRA STODDARD,
*ALEXANDRA STODDARD'S
TEA CELEBRATIONS:
THE WAY TO SERENITY*

Now that you have learned to live with yourself in the kitchen, to feel comfortable with your strengths and limitations as a cook, give it no mind. In a Zen way forget about everything you have accomplished as a preparer of food, at least for the time it takes you to work through this chapter. It will be there anytime you need it.

This part of the book is about *serving* food, about pleasing your guests, it is not about *what* you will prepare, but *how* and *why* you present what you will offer to those who will share a meal with you. This chapter is about meal as ritual, as ceremony, about form that, in a way, takes content for granted. This meal puts the relationships between the host and the guests to the fore because what is served is assumed, is predetermined in a way. This is a moment without pretense, without show. It is following a path rather than creating one. Because so many millions of others have had the same experience in the same way, it is an opportunity to enter this vast, common stream of a shared moment, to know others and to experience the self at the same time.

In the East and in the West the food experience that most strongly emphasizes service as ritual is tea. Conventions, routines, and gestures, the simple ceremony, is more important than the exact nature of the drink and the food. Tea after all is a snack, but a snack with meaning.

THE AFTERNOON TEA PARTY

England is the center of Occidental tea drinking. Tea drinking began there in the 1650s. The afternoon tea was invented by

Anna Maria, the seventh Duchess of Bedford, early in the nineteenth century. The purpose, as she so succinctly stated, was to "combat that sinking feeling" that overwhelmed her every afternoon at about four o'clock.

The English national character, the respectful, dignified, accepting personality we are so familiar with, is largely summed up in the act of drinking tea. In a way, the English sneak up on the significance of the tea ritual by their offhand, casual approach. But they reveal their understanding of its significance by their quiet obsession with accomplishing it *every* day at the *same* time.

In the United States there is a revival of interest in tea drinking, partly because the calming, focused social activity that surrounds tea provides a soothing contrast to the jarring, cup-of-coffee-on-the-run addiction practiced by so many Americans.

The richness of detail in the elements of the tea service provide both reassurance and continuity, and opportunities for self-expression. In the West there is more room for individuality, while the Japanese tea ceremony centers on focused repetition. Balancing these two elements according to individual and cultural needs creates a mindful experience for the host and for the guests. Tea is playful yet serious. Tea is not lunch or breakfast. It is a meal that exists without clear nutritional purpose, which sets the stage for the realization that tea isn't results-oriented. It is a process and therefore should unfold in a leisurely time frame.

To prepare tea in the traditional English manner undertake the following:

1. Fill a kettle with fresh water (filtered or spring if possible).
2. Bring the water to a boil.
3. Heat the pot with a bit of boiling water. Pour it out.
4. Add to the pot 1 teaspoon of loose tea per cup.
5. Fill the teapot. Steep for three to five minutes, depending on your taste.

The traditional tea service is presented on a tray or trays. It is placed around a centerpiece of flowers, usually in the den or the sitting room or on an outdoor patio. The presentation of tea and snacks is arranged in this manner:

1. Cloth napkins and tablecloth are essential touches.
2. The centerpiece is a flower arrangement.
3. Milk or cream is presented in a pitcher.
4. Sugar is in a bowl.
5. Lemon slices are on a small plate with a dessert fork.
6. There are a set of tea cups, saucers, and plates for each guest.
7. Sandwich plates are accompanied by small forks.
8. The strainer and stand have their own plate.
9. There is a waste bowl for tea dregs.
10. Butter is on a small plate with a knife.
11. Jam is in a bowl with a spoon.
12. Clotted cream is in a bowl with a spoon.
13. Hot water is in a covered pitcher.

The traditional tea includes some or all of the following foods according to the adage "something savory, something sweet, always delicious":

1. Finger sandwiches (cucumber, olive spread, smoked salmon, jam are traditional)
2. Scones with jam and clotted cream
3. Pastries—cookies, tarts
4. Loaf or fruit cake
5. Layer cake

The Tea Ritual should unfold with these elements:

1. Greet your guests in a composed manner. Invite them in and make sure that they are comfortable.
2. Go to the kitchen and boil the water. While it is heating, take the food and service to the table on trays.
3. Make the tea and bring it to the table.
4. Ask guests how they take their tea—with milk, with lemon or sugar, or black. If they request milk, add it to the cup before you pour the tea. Offer them sugar and/or lemon. Present each guest with the savories and then the dessert plates.
5. Offer more tea.

THE ROLE OF THE HOST

The host focuses on creating a calm, aesthetically pleasing environment, rich in detail and in comfort. The host offers the most heartfelt gifts of tea and of food as a matter of course. There is no sense of authorship, of taking credit, nor of being in charge. The only expectation the host should have is that the guests will enjoy themselves in each other's company.

THE ROLE OF THE GUEST

The guest should arrive with an open mind, ready and willing to explore all the possibilities of the moment. In this regard we can recall the fantasy element of the invitees to a little girl's tea party. They are supposed to plunge in to the improvisation without hesitation. This is not a networking opportunity. Rather see it as a chance to really learn who is sitting next to you. Come with time on your hands. The worst thing a guest can do is impart a sense of impatience or restlessness. Focus on what is going on around you. It is all you have.

THE JAPANESE TEA CEREMONY

As described below, a typical tea ceremony takes place in an almost dancelike sequence of movements.

Arriving at the host's residence, the guests see that water has been sprinkled in the area of the doorway. This represents an invitation to enter, and as they do so they remove their shoes and hang up their coats. Symbolically, the guests are putting external concerns aside as a first step in the ceremony.

Once inside, the guests pass through a garden to the tea hut. If the home lacks a garden and hut, a hallway from the entrance to the tearoom fulfills the same transitional purpose.

The guests rinse their hands at a specially provided water basin. They then enter the tearoom, ideally through a low door that enforces humility by causing them to look at their feet.

The last guest to enter closes the door just loud enough to let the host know that everyone has arrived. In an adjacent kitchen, the host makes a similarly discreet noise by pouring a little water into a kettle. This signals awareness of the guests' presence.

The host enters the tearoom, bows to his guests, and receives their compliments on the decor of the room and the artfully displayed tea-making utensils. The host then sets about making the fire, a process in which every movement is precisely defined and ritualized from the way in which the charcoal is lit to the exact moment the coals are stirred and the tea kettle placed over the white-hot embers. An incense burner is also lighted, but not before it has been displayed to the guests, who are expected to examine it and offer favorable comments.

The host withdraws to the cooking area, then returns with trays on which a meal of soup, cakes, vegetables, sake, and perhaps some broiled fish are elegantly displayed. Following the meal, the guests briefly return to the garden until the sound of a small gong summons them back into the tearoom.

The tea-making utensils are ritually cleansed in view of the guests. A thick tea is then made by whisking the green leaves in a bowl, which is passed around the room to each guest who takes a sip. Thin tea is then made from the same leaves. This is served in individual cups together with a sweet. Again, the guests comment appreciatively on the utensils.

After showing his guests to the door and bidding them farewell, the host traditionally spends a few moments in reflection upon what has just transpired.

Every ritualized gesture has both practical and symbolic importance. Every movement of the hands, every glance, every taking of food or drink moves the ceremony forward on the physical level, and at the same time creates an allegorical narrative of grace and hospitality.

The ceremony itself is hundreds of years old and has undergone countless refinements. Even the implements have acquired a spiritual glaze. But for Westerners, this austere, minimalist ritual may seem part of some distant world, far removed from our own experience.

It is interesting that both of these serenity rituals, East and West, have developed on islands where space is limited and there is a sense that the intense pressures of claustrophobic living need to be relieved. Today we all share the sense of proximity and intensity the Japanese and the English know well. We are looking for ways to transform our overheated lives into something more peaceful and dignified. Tea can be a part of that process.

A MINDFUL LOOK

A mindful host takes the lead and, along with the guests, participates in forming a larger unity of giving and receiving, creating and appreciating. It is this unity that Alexandra Stoddard calls lingering intimacy. To prepare yourself for the host role, put yourself in the position of the guest as you answer these questions:

1. Describe a dinner party you attended that was memorable for the performance of a giving host.
2. What did the host do to put you at ease? Was it something he or she said? The way the rooms were lit, decorated, and so on? The food that was served, or how it was offered?
3. Did the host seem to be aware of the effect of his approach or was it an "unconscious" graciousness?
4. How did you respond to the host's approach?
5. How did the other guests respond?
6. Describe your relations with the other guests that evening. If you knew any of the guests previously, did this represent a change in your rapport?

A MINDFUL STEP

Now that you have a sense of the range of tea experiences, create a tea service around a theme or with a focus that is important to you. As the host you should focus on your role. You create an atmosphere of conviviality by demonstrating your respect for the details. Spend time arranging a beautiful centerpiece, selecting the appropriate tray and linen, brewing a perfect cup of tea. These are simple acts, simple gestures. Yet they have a way of influencing the tone of the event. Buy the sandwiches and sweets so you can be free to focus on giving ease to the event itself.

Selecting a theme will give you an organizing principle and inspire self-confidence. It can carry through in the choice of foods and in the decoration, even in who is invited. The theme may be nothing more involved than a reunion of friends getting together after an absence, a summer solstice commemoration, the beginning of the school year, and so on. Stay away from celebrations of a business promotion. You know where those conversations are likely to go. Tea is a respite from the relentless pressures of making a living. If you bring your own personality to the ritual, your guests will welcome the interplay between structure and individuality. This dynamic will encourage a sense of freedom and the event will take on a life of its own.

ON THE HORIZON

Create a tea party in which you create your own fusion of the choreographed gestures of the Japanese tea ceremony with the more open-ended style of the English tea service. You may want to take one element from the Japanese service such as the way the guests are greeted, use green tea or Japanese foods, serve a stronger then a weaker tea, or change the tone of the ceremony to a more formal one throughout. You may choose to speak minimally or simply add a different kind of decorative element reminiscent of the Eastern service.

EAST-WEST EGG SALAD
SANDWICHES • *Yields 8 sandwiches*

This recipe is an example of how you can combine Western and Eastern elements of flavor in a single dish. It is a simply made integration of Chinese flavors into a classic English sandwich recipe. It suggests the possibility of fusing the two approaches to tea.

2/3 cup mayonnaise

4 tablespoons rice wine vinegar

1 teaspoon soy sauce

1 tablespoon chopped fresh cilantro

1 tablespoon chopped scallions

1/2 cup chopped canned water chestnuts

1/4 teaspoon five-spice powder

8 hardboiled eggs, chopped

16 slices white bread

Spinach leaves, washed and dried

In a mixing bowl combine the mayonnaise, vinegar, soy sauce, cilantro, scallions, water chestnuts, five-spice powder, and eggs. Mix thoroughly. Cover 8 slices of bread evenly with the egg salad. Arrange spinach leaves to cover on the remaining 8 slices. Form 8 sandwiches. Cut diagonally in two directions to make 32 triangular-shaped pieces. Chill in the refrigerator for an hour covered with plastic wrap.

CHAPTER THIRTEEN

TRANSFORMATION

*Mindful awareness of different options gives
us greater control. This feeling of greater control, in turn, encourages us to be more mindful. Rather than being a chore, mindfulness
engages us in a continuing momentum.*

—ELLEN J. LANGER, *MINDFULNESS*

The Austrian philosopher Ludwig Wittgenstein was a unique
individual in many ways, not least in his attitude toward food.
"I don't care what I eat," he once said, "as long as it's the same
thing every day."

Clearly, Wittgenstein looked somewhere other than the
kitchen for life's pleasures. But for many people food and
cooking seem to become more important every day. What we
choose to eat is now fraught with connotations. Once it was
enough that food should taste good, but now planning a meal
for friends can be an expression of where we stand on nutrition, health issues, and perhaps politics, as well as a reflection
of our financial status. Making "wrong" decisions in culinary
matters can cause severe embarrassment. In late Victorian
times, leaving the legs of a piano exposed was considered

vulgar in polite society. Today, a similar kind of vulgarity is associated with certain kinds of mustard or salad dressing. Ranch dressing, Green Goddess, Thousand Island—these simply aren't tolerated in certain circles! In many ways this sense of status and of embarrassment is the curse of modernism. It has taken us away from the authentic food experience we can all enjoy and substituted something decidedly hierarchical and rarefied.

An important purpose of this book has been to take the labels off cooking's various aspects, to release us even momentarily from these kinds of value judgments and to see ourselves in the kitchen as if for the first time. Mindfulness, with its concentrated focus on process rather than prescribed outcome, is a very powerful tool for accomplishing this end.

In closing I want to relate two food experiences that couldn't be further apart in terms of scale and style. In a way they define the two poles of the mindful experience in terms of material conditions. One was opulent, the other sparse, one sophisticated, the other humble, one self-aware, the other free from self-consciousness. Yet both of them have important aspects of mindfulness at their core, both radiated a respect for their guests through the spirit of generosity that pervaded each meal, both were exactly the right thing to do given the circumstances.

The first was the high point of my catering career. It took place in 1979 in northern California. I was hired by my friend Francis Ford Coppola to organize and prepare an Easter Sunday lamb-and-goat roast for 700 invitees.

This event would occur on the grounds of his Napa Valley

vineyard and estate in the town of Rutherford. For me, working for Coppola was a once-in-a-lifetime chance to undertake
outdoor cooking on a grand scale, to accomplish an engineering feat like building the Suez Canal or the Eiffel Tower. I
had no idea what I was getting into, and that was the appeal
of the project. If I were an artist, it would have been like painting murals on the sides of major public buildings after a career of landscapes and portraits. In short, this was a unique
creative opportunity.

For the host the barbecue represented something very different. Accustomed to making movies, he saw a chance to realize the fantasy of an early Roman or Renaissance banquet
or an Italian wedding feast in all its grandeur unmediated by
film and camera. He saw an opportunity to create every detail of a Sicilian village festival and have his family, friends,
and associates participate in real time. Coppola's movie work
had confirmed his understanding that the meaning is in the
details, the minutiae of a scene. He and his associates
planned this party with the same attention to minutiae.

I had arrived in the Napa Valley two days early to take de-
livery of the fuel—500 pounds of charcoal in fifty-pound
bags, and a cord of wood. The barbecue pit had to be dug—
it was twenty-five feet long and ten feet wide—and the meat
of twenty lambs and ten goats had to be stored.

Weeks earlier, I had contracted for a gigantic metal grill. I
had also hired five assistants, two of whom showed up the day
before the cookout.

The meat was rubbed with olive oil and garlic the night before, then covered in cheesecloth. At 8 A.M., fifty oak logs

were ignited in the bottom of the barbecue pit. They threw off an intense heat that could be felt twenty feet from the fire. When the open flames had subsided, we began cooking the meat over a sea of red ash, with the immense grill some four feet above.

We planned to cook the meat for four hours. The cooks were in constant motion, turning the animals, basting them with red wine, and cutting off tastes for the hungry catering staff. A quarter of a mile away, approaching guests could see plumes of smoke wafting over the big house.

By the appointed hour of 2 P.M., the food was ready to eat. Two eight-foot tables were set up as a carving area, one lamb or goat per table. The sheer physical expanse of this abundance was startling and, for me at least, somehow deeply moving. I felt as though I had been transported back in time to a Renaissance feast with all its pageantry and sense of poetry.

A line of 200 people had already formed in anticipation of the holiday celebration that included dozens of side dishes as well. Carrying twenty pounds of meat at a time, the catering staff moved back and forth between the cutting boards and the food tables. The sounds of silverware and glassware were like an army of crickets. When the last guest had been served some four hours later, I was exhausted, dead on my feet, but happy that we had somehow managed to complete such an all-encompassing undertaking. Nature too had collaborated. The weather had been spectacular, but the next day a torrential spring rain turned the cooking area into a swamp.

As for the second chapter . . . Years ago, in a small seaside town in Mexico, I met some fishermen who had caught half a dozen rather large sharks. After I'd helped load their catch onto the flatbed truck of a local distributor, the fishermen were kind enough to invite me to dinner at the house they all shared. This turned out to be little more than a hut—a single large room without electricity or any furniture whatsoever. The men slept in hammocks hung from the walls, which at least provided protection from whatever might come crawling by during the night. They cooked outside over a charcoal-fueled stove. One of the men made tortillas on a hand press. Another prepared the rice and beans that was to be our dinner.

When it was time to eat, we all sat in a circle on the floor. A bottle of Mescal was passed around, and the food followed. My Spanish was adequate for a simple conversation, and afterward we went outside and talked for a while under the stars. That was a truly memorable dinner. There was something innocent and matter-of-fact about it, and also something sublime. In short, it too was everything cooking should be.

BLACK BEANS • *Serves 4*

These dishes are a bit more complicated than the beans and hot peppers I was served that night. That recipe was lost in the passing bottle of Mescal. Bean recipes are as common as there are cooks who make Mexican food. Here is mine.

. . . .

2 yellow onions, chopped

2 carrots, peeled and chopped

10 cloves garlic, chopped

3 red bell peppers, chopped

3 stalks celery, chopped

1 or more jalapeño or serrano peppers according to taste, chopped

3 tablespoons olive oil

1 pound dried black beans, soaked in cold water for 2 hours

½ cup chopped fresh parsley

½ cup chopped cilantro

2 tablespoons fresh oregano

Salt and pepper to taste

Vegetable or chicken stock

In a pot large enough to hold the beans, sauté the vegetables in oil until soft. Add the black beans, herbs, and salt and pepper. Cover with stock and simmer for 1 hour or until the beans are tender. Prepare white rice by boiling 2 cups of rice in 3 cups of water or stock. Once the liquid has begun to boil, turn down to a simmer and cook for 20 minutes.

Just before you are ready to serve, warm corn or flour tortillas wrapped in foil in a toaster oven or full-size oven. Fill warmed tortillas with rice and beans, and top with guacamole.

MANGO GUACAMOLE • *Serves 4*

3 avocados, peeled and chopped

2 mangoes, peeled and chopped

4 tomatoes, chopped

2 cloves garlic, peeled and chopped

$\frac{1}{2}$ cup chopped fresh cilantro

2 or more jalapeños, chopped

Juice of 3 limes

Salt and pepper to taste

Combine all the ingredients in a bowl. Mix carefully. Refrigerate until ready to serve.

A MINDFUL LOOK — REVISITED

In the opening pages we said that one of the goals of this book is to help you, the reader, become more self-accepting in the kitchen. One way to measure your progress is to return to the self-assessment that concluded the first chapter. Comparing your answers now with what you responded at the outset is a concrete way of marking the distance traveled along a path that doesn't have an end.

1. How do you picture yourself when you cook? Are you relaxed, anxious, hurried, preoccupied? Create a one hundred–word portrait of your kitchen persona listing several things you like and don't like about cooking.

2. How do you imagine others perceive you when you are cooking? Ask a few of your friends to confirm or correct this perception.

3. What do you see as the major obstacles to being more comfortable and effective in the kitchen? Include in this list hang-ups, fears, preoccupations, practical limitations, and so on.

A MINDFUL STEP

In this final exercise we return to where the cooking process begins and ends, with the most ever-present natural representation of transformation—fire. It is the primary force, the basic energy for the process of transmutation we call cooking. Nothing is more primitive, more essential, more fundamental than flame. If anyone needs to be reminded of the power of fire to confer life, think of the frenzied scenes from *Quest for Fire,* the film about primitive people's struggle to survive. The search for flame stood as a poetic and literal testament to humankind's ingenuity and passion to endure.

Recently I watched a documentary on the captivity and escape of an American pilot during the Vietnamese War, *Little Dieter Learns to Fly,* by Werner Herzog. Dieter's guards, Laotian Pathet Lao guerillas, had a problem. They were unable to insure that matches would stay dry in the damp rain forest, especially during the rainy season. To make fire they carried with them an elaborate, hand-carved, interlocking bamboo apparatus that required the full pressure of two men over several minutes to do the job. Smoke billowed up for a minute before a small flame was created. At this point one of the men became the full time custodian of the fire that was never allowed to go out, carrying the now burning charcoal dangling from a long bamboo pole in a small, covered and ventilated iron pot.

Take a few minutes to build a fire the old-fashioned way. You will need: (1) a sunny day, (2) a magnifying glass, (3) some wood shavings to act as kindling, and (4) small logs of any wood. You can do this out in the open, or in a small hibachi on an urban terrace.

Focus the sunlight onto the kindling in a narrow ray with the magnifying glass. Within a few minutes smoke will begin to billow up. When open flames appear add larger pieces of wood. Build a roaring fire. Take a few minutes to sit and look at the flames. Focus on what you have accomplished along the mindful path.

As the fire dies down a bit, take a green stick or a long fork and skewer something—a turkey dog, a marshmallow, a piece of summer squash, or a peach. Roast it in the flames. Enjoy it. You deserve it.

ON THE HORIZON

Six months or a year or two years from now, look back through this book and notice how you have changed since your first reading. Savor that experience. The pleasure of transformation is one of life's greatest joys, yet it is often hard to see.

A GUIDE TO RESOURCES

FARMS

Eckerton Hills Farm, 130 Far View Road, Hamburg,
Pennsylvania, 19526 (610) 562-3591

Fairview Gardens Farms, 598 N. Fairview Avenue, Goleta,
California, 93110 (805) 967-7369

Good Shepherd's Farm, Masonville, New York, 13804
(607) 265-3830

RESTAURANTS

Chez Panisse, 1525 Shattuck Avenue, Berkeley, California,
94709 (510) 548-5049

Frank Restaurant, 88 Second Avenue, New York, New York,
10003 (212) 420-0202

Picasso Café, 359 Bleecker Street, New York, New York
10014 (212) 929-6232

Restaurant Petrelle, 34 rue Petrelle, Paris 10ᵉ, France 4282-
1102

FARMER'S MARKETS

You can find the location of the farmer's market in your area
on the United States Department of Agriculture web site:
www.ams.usda.gov/farmersmarkets

SUGGESTIONS FOR FURTHER READING

Abelman, Michael. *From the Good Earth* (New York: Harry Abrams, 1993).

Assire, Jerome. *The Book of Bread* (Paris: Flammarion, 1996).

Bragg, Gina, and Simon, David. *A Simple Celebration* (New York: Harmony Books, 1997).

Brillat-Savarin, Jean-Anthelme. *The Physiology of Taste* (New York: Penguin Books: 1970).

Chang, K. C. (Ed.). *Food in Chinese Culture* (New Haven, CT: Yale University Press, 1977).

Chopra, Deepak. *Perfect Health* (New York: Harmony Books, 1991).

Chopra, Deepak. *Perfect Weight* (New York: Harmony Books, 1994).

Cossman, Madeline. *Fabulous Feasts: Medieval Cookery and Ceremony* (New York: George Brazillier, 1976).

Dao, Deng-Ming. *Zen: The Art of Modern Eastern Cooking* (San Francisco: Bay Books, 1998).

Dogen and Uchimaya, Kosho. *From the Zen Kitchen to Enlightenment* (New York: Weatherhill, 1983).

Feeley-Harnik, Gillian. *The Lord's Table: The Meaning of Food in Early Judaism and Christianity* (Washington: Smithsonian Institution Press, 1981).

Fletcher, Janet. *Fresh from the Farmer's Market* (San Francisco: Chronicle Books, 1997).

Field, Carol. *Celebrating Italy* (New York: William Morrow, 1990).

Ginzberg, Louis. *Legends of the Bible* (Philadelphia: Jewish Publication Society, 1975).

Glassman, Bernard, and Fields, Rick. *Instructions to the Cook: A Zen Master's Lessons in Living a Life That Matters* (New York: Bell Tower, 1996).

Hanh, Thich Nhat. *The Miracle of Mindfulness* (Boston: Beacon Press, 1975).

Harmon, Willis, and Rheingold, Howard. *Higher Creativity* (Los Angeles: Jeremy Tarcher, 1984).

Huizinga, Johan. *Homo Ludens* (Boston: Beacon Press, 1965).

Kesten, Deborah. *Feeding the Body, Nourishing the Soul* (Berkeley, CA: Conari Press, 1997).

Knight, Elizabeth. *Tea with Friends* (Pownal, VT: Storey Books, 1998).

Langer, Ellen J. *Mindfulness* (Reading, MA: Addison Wesley, 1989).

Lao Tzu. *Tao Te Ching* (New York: Penguin Books, 1989).

Morningstar, Anadea. *The Ayurvedic Cookbook* (Twin Lakes, WI: Lotus Press, 1990).

Nachmanovitch, Stephen. *Free Play* (Los Angeles: J. P. Tarcher, 1991).

Olney, Richard. *Simple French Food* (New York: Atheneum, 1974).

Pettigrew, Jane. *The Tea Companion* (New York: Macmillan, 1997).

Reinhardt, Peter. *Brother Juniper's Bread Book* (Reading, MA: Addison Wesley, 1991).

Root, Waverley. *Eating in America* (New York: William Morrow, 1976).

Root, Waverley. *The Food of France* (New York: Random House, 1958).

Root, Waverley. *The Food of Italy* (New York: Random House, 1971).

Sen, Soshitsu. *Tea Life, Tea Mind* (New York: Weatherhill, 1979).

Stoddard, Alexandra. *Alexandra Stoddard's Tea Celebrations: The Way to Serenity* (New York: William Morrow, 1997).

Tonkinson, Carol (Ed.). *Wake Up and Cook* (New York: Riverhead Books, 1997).

Trager, James. *The Food Chronology* (New York: Henry Holt, 1995).

Trungpa, Chogyam. *Meditation in Action* (Boston: Shambala, 1996).

Visser, Margaret. *Much Depends on Dinner* (New York: Macmillan, 1986).

RECIPE INDEX

In the late 1970s ISAAC CRONIN *was one of the original participants in the California-based New American food movement. His hands-on experience harvesting food includes several years as a commercial fisherman on Monterey Bay. As a specialty produce farmer, he introduced California-grown baby lettuce salad to New York restaurants. Cronin has authored five cookbooks and worked as the marketing director of a cookbook publishing company. He has helped popularize such foods as squid, garlic, and olive oil and regional Chinese cooking. His weekly column on seafood appeared in the* Los Angeles Times *and other California dailies for a number of years. He co-wrote the highly acclaimed independent film* Chan Is Missing, *the first feature directed by Wayne Wang. Cronin is married and the father of two children*